# Becoming
# Masters of Light

# Becoming
# Masters of Light

## Co-Creating the New
## Age of Enlightenment

Darrin William Owens

4th Dimension Press ■ Virginia Beach ■ Virginia

*This book is dedicated to Helen.*
*Thank you for always reminding me of my invincible spirit.*

# Contents

# Acknowledgments

I give all my love and thanks to my soul sister, Jennie Taylor Martin, and the A.R.E. for making a dream come true. To the wonderfully gifted Mary Warren Pinnell for her editing magic and new friendship.

To my family: Carol, Helen, Karen, and Scott. Thank you for the support and the love.

To Carol Pate: Thank you for helping me discover my destiny and for teaching me truth from the very beginning. Your wisdom continues to inspire me.

To H.A.L.: Thank you for your presence and insight, my spirit brother.

Deepest thanks and love to my spirit directors, Master Ron Roth and Her Divine Majesty, Gloriana; you fill my heart and soul with pure wisdom.

# Introduction: The Reluctant Psychic, No More

Since the publication in 2006 of my book, *Reader of Hearts: The Life and Teachings of a Reluctant Psychic,* my life began to take on many forms. I became a published author, a renowned lecturer and spiritual teacher, as well as a celebrity, to some degree. I accepted the majority of the roles I needed to step into, but fame did not sit well with me at all. How could a spiritual teacher be a celebrity? At book signings, I met people from all over the country who had read my book and were literally changed by what they had read in its pages. Helping people was my intent. What was not my intention was the "guru" façade that I felt was manifesting itself at every public appearance I made.

People wanted their pictures taken with me, my autograph, and just to be near me. My concern was that they were seeing me as the source of the message and not just the messenger. I was not the Divine; I was merely delivering the Divine's message. I had a taste of what a true mystic like Edgar Cayce must have experienced in his time–to be not only a deliverer of blessings but also to be looked upon as the blessing itself. I had worked with many "famous" psychics and spiritual teachers during this period and was hoping to find someone with the same challenge I was experiencing. Instead, I found a "Spiritual Hollywood" type of atmosphere. Colleagues who had been my friends prior to my writing the *Reader of Hearts* book were no longer my friends once I became a published author. I was now their competition. To say that I experienced a shock to my system was an understatement. I had the perception that all of us "spiritual celebs" were on the same team and had the same mission: to inspire, to educate, and to heal the planet.

With this new world of "spiritual celebrity showdowns" at my doorstep, I felt pretty much alone in my professional world. I did have the blessing of a few friends in the business, but all in all, it was not a business I felt very inspired by.

Messiah complexes were running rampant. When did the spiritual and self-help "movement" become "Spiritual Hollywood"? I could see that the true soul of a very powerful movement was in jeopardy of losing its purpose. Sadly, in my opinion, the movement was not so much about healing any more as it was about "star gazing." After about two years of pushing my book, giving interviews, and lecturing, I burned out. I stopped. I was experiencing my own personal issues at home dealing with a sour relationship and personal feelings of inadequacy. Yes, even we psychics and spiritual teachers have our issues. I needed a break from my own spotlight. I had to get back to what was real. It was time to re-balance my life and gain a clear perspective on my affairs. I left the psycho-spiritual rat race and stepped into my own cocoon in order to heal. A bitter, unhappy spiritual teacher is a bore. I don't like to be a bore.

What was to be a yearlong hiatus became a three-year retirement. I went back into my work as a publicist and booking agent for speakers. I had done this freelance job between private healing sessions before psychic celebrity fame hit me. It's funny how the Divine will lead us into life experiences that hold all the answers to the question marks we create for ourselves. I ended up as a booking agent for celebrated actresses who had expanded their careers into spiritual teaching and healing. I found the irony fascinating, as I had previously labeled the current spiritual and self-help movement "Spiritual Hollywood." Now, I was booking events for this very same movement. It was, however, a completely different energy.

I coined the term, "conscious celebrity" while working during this time as an agent, which is exactly what these public personalities–whom I had the honor of working with–embodied. The amazing ladies who had been a part of Hollywood for many years advised me repeatedly that it was time for their true work to begin. Their concern was a true eye-opener for me. These lovely ladies of the stage and screen were using their visibility to help people in the pursuit of spiritual healing and guidance. Their helpfulness was the true meaning of Spiritual Hollywood in its most authentic form. A thought that I had cast a shadow on was now transformed into the light that it truly was.

Not only was I working with these ladies but I was also learning from them. I was discovering that millions of people all over the world looked up to them for their show business work and as examples of authentic spiritual individuals, as well. I used to overhear attendees at a workshop with Dee Wallace, Helen Reddy, or Lindsay Wagner proclaim, "If they can balance a "Hollywood" life with their spiritual selves, I can do the same in my own life. I can be balanced, too!" I loved the realization that I detected in people's eyes. I also loved the realization I was seeing within myself, witnessing these Hollywood ladies in all their spiritual glory. During this time, I began to comprehend that my desire for authentic friends and colleagues in the "spiritual biz" came straight out of Hollywood. What divine humor! This timeframe was a wonderful point of enlightenment for me. When I stepped out of the forest, into the sunshine, I could see clearly. I was becoming aware that what I was uncomfortable with during my "psychic celeb years" was something within myself. I had not yet accepted my own mission as a spiritual teacher. So goes the label, "Reluctant Psychic." I was very afraid people would look at me as the divine source and miss the fact that I was only the messenger. In truth, we are all the divine source. As *A Course in Miracles* conveys, we are all ideas in the mind of God. I was forgetting the divine perfection within me. I was forgetting that my mission was to magnify the Divine's love and light on Earth. The very foundation I wanted others to remember was something I had forgotten to reflect within myself. That's what it really boils down to for all of us: we miss the fact that we are divine perfection. What you see in me, you must see within yourself. The reason we walk our spiritual paths is to remember who we truly are. Then, we must magnify, by example, that realization of divinity to the world.

As I write this narrative, it all makes sense. I was not able to receive the gifts from so many people who read my work and listened to my lectures until I was ready to accept the gift of spirit for myself. In truth, I did not take a hiatus from my mission; I went into hiding. I see that now. Thankfully, the soul will never stop its mission of calling us to our highest potential. Now, as with all realization, comes healing and balance. We must be the light God created us to be. As my dear friend, Dee Wallace, often says, "We all have a *bright light*, and we must keep it shining for the world to see, so that we can help others shine, too."

So here I am after three years, and the little voice in my head told me it was time to get back to work. The three years did not pass without working on my own personal issues. I released a relationship that was not good for me, reestablished former friends, built new friendships, and created a wonderful soul family. The reluctant psychic did not feel so reluctant anymore. I was becoming who I was created to be, just like you are. When we truly realize that we are children of the most high, then we start shifting and changing our life to fit that truth. We must clear out the debris and make room for more love in our life. It's a funny thing. Many people still see psychics and spiritual teachers as having all the answers. That is not true at all. We may have "the calling," but we are still souls that inhabit a human body with life lessons to learn just like you. We are in fact, and should be, more reflective than most.

Just because a person writes a book about spirituality does not mean he has fully graduated with honors from his own journey.

It's even more essential for me as a teacher of spirit to delve into my inner questions and walk my talk. Why? The reason is because I cannot in good faith teach you how to rediscover yourself if I'm not doing the same thing. If I don't walk my talk to some degree, I have no justification to tell you how to do it. I have been called the "Judge Judy" of the psychic/spiritual world, a description that I love. But, this comical label comes from the fact that I'll whip myself upside the head with truth just as hard as I would you. We are all in this journey together. This statement is a true and conscious evaluation. The years in which I wrote *Reader of Hearts* and the years that followed its publication were the most expansive for me. I'm still discovering who I am and where I'm going.

It feels good to be with you, dear reader, once more. I'm very excited about my second book. I still get letters from all over the world from fans of *Reader of Hearts*, and they always end their gratitude with, "When is the new book coming out?" Well, kids, here it is. I realize now that it was not the lack of support in the "spiritual business" that was the problem. It was the lack of support from me that was blocking my mission. What we have blocking us within will project itself to our outside world. What we believe within us we will manifest without. Once I truly started supporting myself, spiritually, I attracted people and experiences that would do the same for my life.

If you lack support for yourself, you will draw to you those who agree with you. If you are tired of people who do not support you, start supporting yourself. Then watch the magic happen. We all need a spiritual support group in life. Start a group, but support yourself in the meantime. The Divine will add members to it one by one. Create your own world, and stop living in others' realities. As Judy Garland once said, "Always be a first rate version of yourself and not a second rate version of someone else."

# THIS BOOK: ITS PURPOSE AND USE

Well, Darrin is back and in full spiritual force. It's the dawn of a New Golden Age of Enlightenment, kids, and we have work to do—so let's get to it.

If you have not read my first book *Reader of Hearts: The Life and Teachings of a Reluctant Psychic*, you may want pick it up and give it a go. I wrote it for the purpose of helping people understand the levels of spiritual growth that we all navigate as well as the true role of being psychic. Think of my first book as lubricating your spiritual muscles and this new work as putting those muscles into action.

The purpose of *Becoming Masters of Light: Co-Creating the New Age of Enlightenment* is to focus on how we can utilize our spiritual potential in this new era of consciousness. I will describe the spiritual evolution of psychic potential from as far back as the Old Testament to the present. Also discussed will be how we can release our "need to know" the future in order to embrace the reality that we will co-create. I want to share with you the many spiritual powers and metaphysical systems of healing that I have worked with for many years, because I feel that everyone should open up to these powerful remedies. It's time to be masters of our destiny.

We have been in "metaphysics 101" long enough. We have what we need to fully embrace our divine selves and take hold of the truth that we are the New Earth that we are so longing to see. We are the New Golden Age of Enlightenment. We must stop focusing on the doom–and–gloom nonsense of fear that some are trying to catapult into the atmosphere of our minds. We will stop the thought of fear by not believing in it. Only Love is real. In essence the Shift, the New Golden Age, is not about catastrophe and chaos. Who wants to buy into that reality? It is about the realization and manifestation of a global family. Spiritual humanitarianism is a new foundation that is being birthed from all of us that are heeding the call to heal our planet.

This is a book is for the conscious soul. It's a primer on the spiritual powers available to us as master co-creators with the Divine. Along with a retrospective on the evolution of our soul's progression insofar as psychic power and spiritual healing, it also covers a wide range of subjects formulated to enhance the spiritual resources within you. My goal for this work is to help you strengthen your inner foundation with the Mother/Father God, the Source of all things. As we have crossed the threshold past the year 2012 into the New Golden Age, it's imperative that we be as internally vibrant as possible to represent Mother/Father God on Earth. Instead of looking to others we think are "spiritually special" to be our voices for God on Earth, we must now step into the role of using our own voice of God for ourselves and others. Being a Master of Light means that we are ready and able to be authentic channels of healing and balance. When we master that potential in our own lives, we are better equipped to co-create with the Divine. Is this not the goal of any spiritual journey?

I believe that there is a threefold process to our soul's evolution, in this most sacred timeframe. First, we must awaken to our spiritual selves. Second, we need to allow the awakening of the spiritual reality within to transform us. Third, from that transformation, we will magnify our spiritual foundation as children of the most high. For the conscious soul, it's a time of magnification–to live the spiritual life not as a hobby, but as a lifestyle.

This book is not intended to be a scholarly work on metaphysics or spiritual healing. It's simply a primer, an expansion from my work in *Reader of Hearts*. It's a guide for those who have awakened and transformed and are ready to progress even further into spiritual humanitarianism. From that awareness, we will go a step further into the magnification of our spiritual power. I will present the many mystical and spiritual principles that I have discovered along the way in my professional career as a psychic healer, as well as in my own personal growth. We are lights among the world; and as lights, we must take the responsibility of being co-creators with the source to the fullest degree. From that powerful responsibility, we will learn how to use our spiritual gifts for the benefit of conscious evolution and total well-being for our planet. I know that these are bold statements from an author, but I write these powerful words because I know them to represent truth. Each of you reading this book at this very moment knows there is something more for you to do as a co-creator with God. This book will be your guide to enhance your spiritual self-esteem and reinforce your foundation as an expression of divinity–as a master of light!

"I want to do more!" I hear this call from many of my clients and students, so it is my hope that this book will be an answer to your request. I'm not here to tell you how to get a cool, new age job or how to become a world sensation as a spiritual guru. I'm here to give you information about how to empower yourself and be the best at what you're doing right now. When you feel you are in sync with yourself and the Divine, you are more apt to be open to the living guidance God offers you. You are also–by sensing your own inner security–more open to help and guide others who are currently struggling with their faith and place in the universe. Like moths to a flame, people who are lost in their own unconsciousness will be attracted to your light. You will help others find their own glimmer of truth. Is that not the reason we started our spiritual journeys: not only for our own well-being but also for the well-being of others? The Master Jesus knew early on what his mission was. He did not study with the mystics of his time purely for his own benefit. He studied to strengthen his connection to the Father/Mother God and to prepare his inner dynamics for the responsibility of bringing truth to the masses. As Jesus expressed, as He could do, so can you.

This book will cover many of the spiritual resources we have at hand. I will put my own spin on some subjects with the hope that it will help you to grow even closer to alignment with your spiritual power. I'll refer to master teachers and healers such as Ron Roth, Edgar Cayce, and of course, Jesus. I'll also include the importance of the role of the Divine Feminine, which I lovingly call the Holy Spirit. Another important goal of this work is to understand the evolutionary process of psychic power.

Many of us have become caught in a psychic web, sustaining a sense of desperation to know what's going to happen in our lives or what's around the next corner. There is power and faith in the mystery. Being able to have faith in mystery creates a wellspring of freedom that is our sustenance in remaining connected to the Divine. This ego mind with its fear of the "unknown" has kept many of us away from our ability to be co-creators.

## THE SEVEN LEVELS OF SPIRITUAL GROWTH:
## A QUICK OVERVIEW

Over many years of working with clients and students (and myself!), I've seen a common pattern of spiritual development. Many people go through particular stages in a certain order. Learning the lessons of one stage is what prepares you to advance to the next stage. Once you have downloaded one piece of divine inspiration, you are ready for the next.

The common pattern is to pass through seven different stages, which can be called *spiritual awakening, divine darkness, interior power, inner attunement, conscious creation, holistic living,* and *divine oneness.*

Each of these seven levels of spiritual awareness formulates a progressive expansion for your soul to maintain and magnify its inner awareness as a child of God. It is important be aware of these levels in our lives, and the awareness builds a stronger relationship with the Divine. Even for the conscious soul, these levels of awareness make their presence known in our lives as reminders of our spiritual power. You don't graduate after you experience their lessons–instead, you liberate your soul by the pervasive, ongoing awareness in your life.

## SPIRITUAL AWAKENING

Spiritual awakening is the beginning of the journey of self-discovery. It happens when you begin to see a sliver of the Divine in your life. It's as if your spiritual eyes begin to open from a deep sleep, just enough to see the new morning light. When the awakening process is complete and your spiritual eyes are fully open, you are conscious of your divine nature. You know that there is a divine purpose in everything.

## DIVINE DARKNESS

Once awakening sheds light on what needs to change in your life, you are ready for divine darkness or "the dark night of the soul" to help you make those changes. If awakening happens when you open your spiritual eyes, then divine darkness occurs when you wipe the "sleep" from them. It happens when you begin to cleanse those crusty, irritating habits, illusions, and thoughts that previously glued together your spiritual eyelids. This is the stage of growth that prepares the way for you to clear out anything that keeps you from remembering your true divinity.

## INTERIOR POWER

Once you have cleansed your soul of the illusions that have limited you, you are ready to ascend out of the darkness. Now that you understand the source of divinity, you can move toward the light by learning how to access the energy of the Divine. This energy is all around us, vibrating through our bodies and all matter. You simply have to become more aware of it as you understand how to use it in your spiritual development.

## INNER ATTUNEMENT

You've probably heard the statement *the kingdom of heaven is within*. In this level, you acquire the skills that make this statement a reality in your life. You create a peaceful "inner heaven" by working with the divine energy flowing throughout your body–the energy you discovered from the previous level of awareness. You control, balance, and tune this energy to bring clarity, calm, and a heart–centered focus. This process of inner attunement allows you to maintain your interior power, strengthen your connection to the Divine, and continue on the path of spiritual growth. It gives you a fresh wellspring of energy to invest in your life.

## CONSCIOUS CREATION

*We create our own reality.* This statement has been one of the most popular–and most misunderstood–teachings in the New Age. But the truth it expresses is fundamental to spiritual development. We are creative beings, and our minds are powerful. What we create in our minds shapes our experience of the world, and even the world itself.

It all hinges on your perception–how you see yourself, your situations, and the world you are living in. A person who sees herself as a desirable and successful person in a world of opportunities is going to create around herself a reality that's very different from the reality of a person who thinks of himself as a failure in a world intent on beating him down. Your perception shapes your thinking, your thinking shapes the way you act, the way you act affects the people around you; and it is all reflected back to you.

## HOLISTIC LIVING

Throughout the previous levels, I focused on sustaining and cultivating the inner life of soul development. You have learned that inner attention, when focused correctly, develops your capacities for self-knowledge and communion with the Divine. In this level, you express those spiritual dynamics outward in order to create a lifestyle aligned with your renewed sense of being. In this way, you become a clear channel of divine expression. Once you establish a bond with the Divine, you are meant to express that divinity, to become a channel of peace, and to share your light with others.

## DIVINE ONENESS

The previous levels of spiritual growth led you toward a single goal: to be at one with yourself, the divine presence, and everything around you. This is the experience of *oneness*, of being completely in sync with the sacred energy of the universe. Oneness happens when the real you–your higher self–is fully present at every moment, and when your mind, body, emotions, soul, spirit, and psyche are all in unison with the Divine.

These stages manifest differently for each person. Not everyone goes through them in the same order. And more importantly, once you pass through one "stage" and into another, you aren't necessarily finished with the earlier one. You can be well into the sixth stage but still have to deal with issues you thought you had mastered in the fourth stage. In other words, the stages might be simultaneous. The elements contain lifelong lessons that you will continue to experience from time to time. It's important to remember that spiritual growth is not a contest to be won. You become more and more conscious on many different levels throughout your life. The universe is a vast array of spiritual wisdom that is hidden in every cosmic molecule of life.

Perhaps many of you who are perusing these levels have been nodding your head in alignment to your truth; every soul that opens to its spiritual nature begins the process of these seven levels of consciousness. This new work takes you even further into the co-creative process as a conscious spiritual being. We are truly in the age of accepting the sovereign role of becoming a Master of Light.

## FINAL THOUGHTS

It takes great courage to take the first step on your spiritual journey. It takes even greater courage to continue to experience your spiritual journey. This book is about living your spiritual journey and embodying your role as a true spiritual catalyst while also activating your spiritual power. As you can agree now in 2013, we are still here on the earth. There is obviously more to be done. 2012 was simply an open door into another level of evolutionary consciousness for this planet. The role of this book is to encourage perceiving your life from within while reducing perceptions that are focused "out there." Our empowerment and our perceptions are fed from the energy vibrating within us. Understanding our inner energy changes the way we look at everything in our lives.

Throughout this work, I will include invocations and prayers to help you awaken the deeper spiritual powers that you will be reading about. When we absorb the knowledge of any spiritual work, the use of prayer and invocations while we study can call forth the wisdom enveloped in the teachings. Each chapter will be a subject unto itself. I find that distinct chapters and subjects make it easy for the reader to flip to different topics in order to revisit their message. I have also included recommended books and resources throughout this book to help further your studies and spiritual education. Enjoy the journey—awaken, transform, and magnify!

# The New Golden Age: Becoming Masters of Light

There is absolutely no doubt that we are experiencing a new and more dynamic dimension of reality, but we must fully realize that this shift—this change—is manifesting through us. We are the Shift and we are the New Earth.

*News flash!* 2012 has come and gone and we are still living in the present time. It's funny how that happened. Yes, we are still here; and aliens did not come to earth to beam us up to a fantasized, "holier-than-thou," new age earth plane. Our planet did not blow up like a ticking time bomb, no matter what Hollywood tried to portray. We are here because we still have work to do. We exist to help with the spiritual evolution of our global mind by the conscious use of our spiritual and psychic power. We are here because we are stepping into our new role of being ministers of light. If you are reading this book, you are one of the cherished souls chosen to help in this holy quickening.

## LIVING LIFE IN THE NEW GOLDEN AGE

We are living at an incredible time; there is no doubt about that. This is a sacred time where the cosmos takes a sigh of deep, peaceful release, and we are imbued with its nourishment and well-being. Speaking "energetically," we are rising higher in our thought patterns and vibrations. This high vibrational living is the new wave of a more holistic lifestyle that is essential for us to incorporate on a daily basis. Meditation, prayer, and inner attunement are as indispensable as drinking water. I have always taught my students and clients the importance of keeping the physical body in shape and exercising the spiritual body, as well. This new era of our spiritual existence is asking us to embody our spiritual nature as a priority in everything we do. Luckily, as conscious souls, we understand the new spiritual dynamics of healthy living, healthy thinking, and healthy relationships. I won't bore you with more details, as there are many books in the new age market that delve into those subjects. Honestly, by now, you should have gotten the memo! I want to take you a step farther. Again, we are focusing more on spiritual humanitarianism here and less on what can I create, what can I acquire, and who can I attract as an individual? It's "we" time.

## MASTERS OF LIGHT

I'm going to take another bold step at this time. I like doing that often; it keeps my readers on their toes. I'm asking for you to accept a new role. This is a role that takes great courage, backbone, and guts. I assume that if you have read this far and have not yet asked for a refund on this book, you are willing. For the past several years, the global mind has been infused with teachings about the creation of your own reality and the law of attraction. This wonderful progression for the awakening of our planet has taken us only so far. Now, the bold step is to fully understand what creating your reality is truly about. The proper phrase in the New Golden Age is co-creating your reality. You can't co-create without a creative source. That Source is God. Call it what you will—the Universe, Divine Love, or Great Spirit—it is still the very essence of creation. We are temples for this creative spark. Through the teachings of the law of attraction, we were able to partially tap into our creative ability—but only partially. We learned that thoughts are truly things and that with enough intention we could set the stage for what we want.

Sadly, I saw the old ego step in when people began to be preoccupied with creation on a material level.

"Dear God: I want a car, a house, a lover, and a good job."

Don't get me wrong, these requests are just fine. God is glad to provide us with all we desire, but there is a need for balance. I began to feel that we were using our creative energy more to obtain "stuff" and less for the true purpose of co-creation as examples of spiritual humanitarians. We got into this same trouble eons ago when we separated ourselves from the Source and decided to create without the Creator. So entered the great fall of man from God. I write more about that idea later in the book.

I listened as I heard students and clients struggle with manifestation.

"I say my affirmations for a new love twenty times a day, and nothing happens." "Why can't I get a new job? I'm so unhappy; when I put my intention out, there is dead silence."

Honestly, folks, If I were God and I had to hear all of your "I want, I want, I wants," I would take the phone off the hook, too. Think of it this way. You're in your car driving down the highway of life. God is driving and you are the passenger. Remember, you are a co-creator. God knows your direction, knows the turns, and knows the way.

You, on the other hand, like a spoiled child, keep bugging the driver with, "Are we there yet, are we there yet?" "I'm bored, can we pull over?" "Let me drive, let me drive. You're not going fast enough!"

You know how annoying that can be. So, the universe will keep taking you to your destination, but you have missed the mark for your journey. You are so worried about getting there, and having what you want when you want it, that you have lost the true meaning of what it is to be a co-creator with the Divine.

God knows our needs and desires. The true art of manifestation is to set our intentions with God and let everything else go. There is no need for a reminder. In the meantime, we must step into a higher place of co-creating as Masters of Light. It sounds simple, because it is. God is simple.

When our lives feel chaotic, we often remove our focus from our co-creative power. Instead, we put our focus on our ego, consisting of fear and attachment. Remember, it's time to move beyond *me* to *us*.

As we step into the role of a Master of Light, we move into the most powerful level of co-creation. We have set our intentions for a healthy life, full of abundance, and now we must place that life with the Source. The power of surrender is the key. We set our sights on becoming an embodiment of light. We are living in a timeframe where many are still trying to catch up with their own spiritual selves. As burning examples of God's light, we can be there for the handoff. We become extensions of God's divine love and are able to help guide others to their own truth and well-being. All that "stuff" we want comes with ease when we let go of our attachment to it. Beware of new age thought that believes in order to create, you have to attach. Some call it focus; I call it obsessive-compulsive behavior. When you are saying twenty affirmations a day and have poster boards all over your room that reflect the lifestyles of the rich and famous, you're attached instead of creating. You don't need any of that nonsense. God knows your desires before you can even utter them. Proclaim them once to the universe and then let it go. You have bigger fish to fry out in the world as a Master of Light!

A Master of Light is an embodiment of God's pure, divine love on earth. You will also become conscious of the spiritual power running through your being. Remember that. When you truly live by charity, faith, and peaceful action, you are going to shift the actions of many folks around you. You don't need to stand on a corner and shout that you have the truth and the way. God will send you the people and resources you need to be a light for the world. Just as we have had that same blessing in our own life (of meeting the right person at the right time), we now have to be the right person for someone else. This book will cover many subjects to help you open to your Master of Light role. You are ready to take action now, and it is my hope that this little primer will support a deepening of this holy experience.

Remember that our thoughts are things. If we set our thoughts on God, surrendering our desires and needs in order to receive from the Source, we cannot go wrong. We need to keep our mind on our responsibilities as light bearers, and then everything else will be laid before us.

Think of surrendering to God as the best type of job with the best insurance available in the universe. The job perks are limitless.

## MEDITATION FOR A MASTER OF LIGHT

Allow yourself to relax. Take three deep breaths: one for the mind, one for the body, and one for the spirit. Feel your tensions wash away with each breath. Now, just breathe deeply and easily. Still relaxing, let the intake and out breath create a peaceful center within you. Relax. Relax more.

Within your mind, imagine a tiny ball of white light. Allow the light to expand, like a sunrise over the mountaintops. The light becomes larger and larger, and it completely embraces your entire body. You feel the warmth and comfort from this shining white light. Every cell, organ, and bone is bathed completely—refreshed and renewed. The light begins to magnify even more, stretching itself outward from your physical body. Rays of white light expand and grow in every direction. You begin to feel at one with everything and everyone around you. A ray of light directed from your very being reaches out and touches the heart of every individual you come into contact with. You are a lighthouse, a guide for all who see your shining brilliance. You are a Master of Light.

As you take a few more deep breaths, you allow the light rays to play their part in your life. Bring your attention back to your inner self—you are still fully relaxed and still breathing. Take another deep breath and allow yourself to come back to the space where you are. Open your eyes.

Now you can take this inner light out into your day, every day, and embrace the role of being a Master of Light.

# 2 Psychic Intuition: The Evolutionary Power of Our Spiritual Gifts

*O*ver the years, I have written and talked about the essential aspects of psychic power and intuition. First, both of these aspects of our spiritual power work hand in hand. Since we as a global consciousness have evolved and opened more fully to our inner resources, these abilities have become even more magnified within our psyches. I have seen an interesting shift in the perception of what being psychic means to my students and clients. My instruction of psychic power as a spiritual attribute is finally making it into people's belief systems, even though it has been a standard truth for many years. I have always been an advocate of teaching that psychic power is a spiritual gift of the soul and not a circus sideshow. Sadly, through the years, there has been a bad reputation spun around anything that is psychic or intuitive in nature. Back in my hometown, in the Ozarks of Arkansas, it was believed by most people that any psychic subject had been spawned by Satan. Another major misguided point of view was the perception of "psychic" as merely a gypsy fortune-telling trade. This misperception is largely due to bad, B-rated films, the television, phone psychic trade, and other media's reactions to misguided attempts from celebrity psychics looking to shine in the spotlight with their magic powers.

"The psychic, then, is of the soul . . . " (Edgar Cayce reading 5752-1) The Edgar Cayce readings stated it very clearly, and I as a psychic healer have always based my teachings on this simple but powerful truth: being psychic belongs to the soul. Since we are all souls, then we are all endowed with psychic potential. Being psychic is not a "special" gift given to only a few, therefore; it is part of the spiritual makeup of every soul. As our soul evolves, our psychic potential evolves, and we are becoming vastly multidimensional. This evolution is for the conscious soul that has become aware of its spiritual power. He or she asks the question that I hear so often now: "What's next?" The next step in psychic awareness is the understanding of what we can do in helping the "shift" of our planet by using our psychic intuitive power.

First, let me describe the union between psychic power and intuition. I want to give you a clear picture of the resources within you. I teach that we are all psychic intuitives because all of us carry both senses. Some folks think that people are endowed with either one or the other of these spiritual powers or that psychic power is better or stronger than intuition. Let me dispel some of that confusion.

There are two questions I am most often asked by students during my workshops.

1.   Am I a psychic or an intuitive?
2.   Is there a difference between the two terms?

My answer to both questions is a definitive yes. Yes, you are both psychic and intuitive, and yes, there is a *huge* difference between the two terms. They do, however, work hand in hand with each other.

Think of the term psychic as being an extended level of intuition. Intuition is like an energy language of the soul. It is an extra sense that is more personal in nature for an individual. It's a whisper from your higher self. Think of intuition as information that is directed internally. Intuition fuels many spiritual tools such as energy healing, hunches, gut feelings, meditative awareness, and creativity.

Subtle power is the nature of intuition. Intuition always directs us back to ourselves. It also gives us helpful information for our life's path. The psychic nature is more extroverted and impersonal in its energetic intelligence. It is a magnification of intuitive awareness in the process of accessing energy from others and the environment. Psychic power is the ability to access information from energy and intelligences outside of one's inner personal dynamics. Psychic ability encompasses the gifts of reading others intuitively, communicating with the dead, accessing potential future realities, and having medical clairvoyance. These are all psychic powers, just to name a few.

Intuition is more personal while psychic ability is more impersonal in accessing energetic information. You can also think of psychic ability as the expanded mind that accesses energetic information, whereas intuition is the key used in the clear and accurate interpretation of the energetic information. When I conduct my healing sessions, I'll see a vision or get an impression of my client, psychically. Then I run it through my intuition by asking: what does this information mean for my client? By simply asking a question, I have given my intuition permission to access the personal results of the psychic vision. That's why many people have visions or psychic flashes about something but never think to ask their intuition for its clarity about them. They are so hung up on the "glamour" of the vision that they have forgotten to ask their intuition for its meaning and direction. I see many psychic people out there who talk to the dead or psychically tap into people with great accuracy, but they are missing one thing. They lack a spiritual connection to their intuitive voice. Remember, intuition is your direct communication link from your higher self. So many people who are psychic are truly talented, but their information has no sustenance at all because they are not asking for the deeper meanings. Some, mostly healers and counselors, are highly intuitive about feeling people's emotions and their pain. By asking your psychic self to elaborate, you can receive the actual visions of the situations in that person's life that may have caused the "dis-eased" feelings. I hope you can now understand the essential union of both psychic and intuitive powers. You can see a great example of the union of psychic intuition with medical intuitives. They're able to psychically see the diseased area of the body, and through their intuitive connection, they are able to get information about why the diseased organ has manifested in the body. Like I always say, trying to be "psychic" without a strong spiritual and intuitive foundation is like living in Wisconsin with a lactose intolerance problem. Enough said!

## THE EVOLUTION OF PSYCHIC INTUITION

Let's begin with an evolutionary scale of spiritual power from its prophetic nature in the biblical Old Testament to its renewed force as a healing agent today. I believe we are presently realizing the true source of psychic intuition as an expanded sense for healing and well-being. I'm using the time scale according to the Bible because I believe these scriptures have demonstrated an incredible account of psychic power through the ages right up to the embodiment of the Christ when psychic ability became conscious as a spiritual element to be awakened within every soul. I'll overlay the evolution of spiritual power via the chakra system, as well.

The chakra system, or our energy anatomy, cycles and recycles energy throughout our body. It is also an historical account of our psychic growth throughout time. Just as the rings of a tree indicate its history and growth, so does our energy system reflect the same for us.

Our energy system is an incredible textbook of inner knowledge of the origin and even the destiny of our soul's growth.

In his book, *Edgar Cayce: Reflections on the Path*, Herbert Puryear, writes on page 119:

> We know also that the body is the temple, where we are to meet God within; it is also a specially constructed instrument for becoming aware of our oneness with God and with all his manifestations in the universe. The growth of insight from the Old Testament to the New Testament is a movement away from the projection of God "out there" toward awareness of his existence within the temple of the Body.

From this statement we enter into the living energy dynamics within us. I'll cover the chakra system, for those who need a quick refresher.

## THE CHAKRA SYSTEM: OUR ENERGETIC ANATOMY

Adapted from *Reader of Hearts* by this author, "Chapter 5: Interior Power and Sacred Energy," (pp. 61–71).

Divine energy is the universal force that keeps everything in motion and breathes life into all beings. It is recognized in all the world's religious and mystical traditions—as the life force, prana, chi, or the creative energy of God. Our bodies and minds were created to be the manifesters, projectors, and controllers of this sacred energy.

The Divine expresses itself as energy within us. This energy is the soul. Our physical body acts as a temple to this energy, as a place for divine energy to flow and vibrate. It's possible to map how divine energy moves within the body, how it manifests itself in different ways in different locations. This is our spiritual anatomy—or energy anatomy. The human spiritual anatomy has been understood for a very long time. As early as 2000 BC, the ancient Hindus had already mapped it out in the form of the chakra system. A chakra is an energy center in the body. Seven of these energy centers align vertically along the spinal column. *Chakra* means "wheel," so we have seven wheels of spinning energy from the base of the spine (the first chakra) to the top of the head (the seventh chakra). Each chakra corresponds to one of the seven colors of the rainbow and each vibrates to one of the seven notes of the musical scale. I and many other psychics and healers have seen the colors and felt the tones vibrating within the human body. Each chakra is associated with a certain part of the body and a certain organ. These seven power centers reflect not only your physical health but also your psychological, emotional, and spiritual state. Each chakra also corresponds to a specific aspect of being.

The lower three chakras are associated with physical needs, the fundamental emotions, and the ego. The third chakra, for example, is the center for self-esteem and personal power. The upper four chakras have a connection to our higher emotional and spiritual faculties.

| Chakra | Location | Color | Life Issue |
|--------|----------|-------|------------|
| First | Base of spine | Red | Grounding and physical security |
| Second | Sexual organs | Orange | Sexuality, money, creativity, and relationships |
| Third | Solar plexus | Yellow | Self-esteem, personal power, courage, and honor |
| Fourth | Heart/chest | Green | Love, forgiveness, and emotional health |
| Fifth | Throat | Blue | Surrender, choice, will, and expression |
| Sixth | Forehead | Indigo | Mystical vision, spiritual intellect, and truth |
| Seventh | Crown | Violet | Connection to the Divine |

To further your education on the chakra system, please see the resources at the end of this book. Next, I will combine the metaphysical principles of the energy anatomy with the psychic evolution of our souls as reflected within the Bible.

## THE SOUL'S PSYCHIC AND SPIRITUAL ORIGINS

Since the creation of our souls, we have been endowed with the same creative potential as the Creator. As the Divine extended itself into countless expressions, called souls, we became companions to God and walked side by side with the Creator, angelic hierarchies, and other divine beings. According to the Cayce readings, a time came when a number of souls decided it would be fun to perform their own creations in the universe, away from God. That was not smart! Trapped in our own rebelliousness and materialistic creations that became our balls and chains, a great sleep fell over our inner eyes. Since that time, we have been "playing in the fields of the Lord" in a way, trying to survive in competition with the source of all being. By God's grace, we were given the example of the Christ ideal to follow and embody so that we might return back to oneness. As we look back, we can see our evolutionary process as it pertains to spiritual power. Beginning with the Old Testament and looking at the time of Moses, our consciousness was rock hard—not unlike the Ten Commandments. The commandments represented our need at that time to understand God as an outside force. We needed prophets and holy men to educate us about God's will and his commandments for us. It was a time of burning bushes, holy voices, and visions. As we progressed, the universe continued to educate us by delivering to us those who expressed the voice of God on Earth.

Holy men during this time also began to prophesy the one true master who would incarnate and give birth to a new way of inner knowing and spiritual understanding. At that time, we, along with a global consciousness, became ready for the appearance of Jesus, the Christ. Once again, we experienced a "time jump" in our inner awakening. We heard the voice and teachings of a man ministering the truth that God was indeed within man. We finally arrived at the next step in our spiritual power. We began to realize that we were indeed children of the most high and not separate from divinity. Then we were taught that we had the same creative potentials within us as the Divine. Jesus the Christ became the supreme ideal for mankind to fully realize the God–Source within.

Through his demonstration of miracles, healings, and teachings, Jesus began to show us the way to truth in connecting to God on our own and using our spiritual co-creative powers for the purpose of realization and healing.

You can do as I can do, Jesus taught. The kingdom of heaven is within, and you can now communicate directly with the Holy Father/Mother God. This idea was truly a huge shift in man's perception. Since then, we continued to struggle to understand and navigate the many mansions of spiritual power within us. Removing the religious dogma and releasing the true teachings of Christ, we have learned that we are imprinted with the same creative intelligence blessed on us many, many eons ago at the dawn of creation. Now, we live in a time of remembrance of our divinity. We can take ourselves to the deepest level of awareness and realize that the power of our psychic intuition is being concentrated back to its fundamental and original purpose—that of healing and spiritual liberation.

If we take a look at the energy scale of the chakra system, we can perceive that the inner evaluation of our soul's psychic nature was reflected directly outward into physical existence. For instance, in the time of the Old Testament with the Ten Commandments as our spiritual ideal, we lived and navigated primarily from the first three chakras: the root, sacral, and solar plexus. All three chakras navigate a more outward approach to living. Chakras one, two, and three deal with issues of our physical existence, tribal law, sex, and also religion. I state religion here because religion tends to represent a tribal association to spirituality; God is still a force out there that must be sacrificed to and appeased. The Old Testament is loaded with stories of people who sacrificed animals to the heavens. This lower chakra consciousness represents a need to bargain with God.

Some folks still make sacrifices to God. "Dear God, if you give me what I want, I'll stop drinking or I'll stop gossiping so much." That kind of consciousness is vibrating to a belief in a separation from the Source. People who bargain with the Creator have yet to understand their co-creative potential. At this point in history, as far as the Old Testament period of time, we had not yet truly grasped the truth of *God* within us. Some of us are still living in forgetfulness of our creative divinity.

Therefore, the Creator blessed and directed holy seers and masters to lead us through the symbolic desert of the unconscious to witness miracles of God's realty through signs and wonders. In essence, the evolutions of the first three chakras were the opening of the gate to perceive the reality of spiritual power and its source. Our next transition was opened with our heart chakra. This was the awakening of the Christ Consciousness.

## CHRIST CONSCIOUSNESS: THE OPENING
## OF THE HEART CHAKRA

As our spiritual evolution progressed, the global mind was fully realized via the opening of the heart chakra. This evolution took place with the life and death of the master, Jesus. His teachings filled the hearts of men, women, and children with the truth that God was within them and that forgiveness was the key to liberating their lives from fear. So, we became empathic, in a sense. We began to grow in consciousness of other people's feelings and emotions. We unlocked the door to our own emotional intelligence. Empathy was a powerful leap in liberating our full potential as psychic intuitive beings. I believe that our intuitive natures were born at this point. From the awakening of the Christ Consciousness, via the crucifixion and resurrection of Jesus, we began to look at our own life and the lives of others more personally. We began to take a look within, where the kingdom of heaven resided. We no longer needed the tribal belief that God was outside of us. It was time, in our spiritual evolution, to go within.

The Christ Consciousness denotes complete union with the Divine. God graced us with a new blueprint to help all souls learn and grow and return back to the source. The Christ gave us an ideal to follow and a ruler by which to measure our life. With this new regimen of enlightenment, we began to focus on the creative divinity within us in order to make better choices. Those choices were based on love that would keep pushing us back to God's perfect reality. Remember, we lost our hats when we separated ourselves from the Source. By the example of Jesus Christ, we would actually begin embodying that same divine consciousness within ourselves in order to return home someday. I'm talking about this process as a metaphysical principle, not as a dogmatic religious teaching. You can be a pagan, Buddhist, or Jewish and still be open to divine union. I just happen to call it Christ Consciousness because Jesus was the master who initiated this truth on earth. The heart chakra opened and a bridge was finally formed between our lower and higher selves. At that time, unity with God was reinstated.

## DIVINE REVELATION: THE OPENING
## OF THE HIGHER CHAKRAS

We have come to the full embodiment of our spiritual evolution with the opening of the next three chakras: the throat chakra, the third eye chakra, and the crown chakra. Believe it or not, many of us are still working on these higher vibrations. I have seen many books on the market about other chakras beyond the seven needing to be activated, and I say, "Hold on!" We are still in need of fully realizing our power within these upper centers. Let's not jump all the way from "a to z" just yet.

Since the resurrection of the Christ Consciousness, our world continues to play a balancing act with Christ's teachings on love, charity, and forgiveness. The opening of the heart was truly an amazing burst of power for man, and it was an influential catalyst, as well. It opened our ability to infuse emotion and passion into what we project and create. So again, the test of love or fear was even more apparent. Are you going to invest your emotion—the power of the heart—in anger and rage, or will you concentrate on love, forgiveness, and union? We are still working on that inner dynamic even now. I believe that the current dawning of the Golden Age will occur when we are ready to begin the experience and direction of the three higher chakras. The fifth, or the throat chakra, represents our communication to the work, or the expression, of who we are. We have recently seen the growth of that power as the global mind has expressed its voice against hate crimes, built the occupy movement, and called for peace among peoples and nations. We have been marching and using our voice against injustice for many years, and we are not seeing another upheaval in this process. Thank God!

The third eye and crown chakras represent our co-creative and spiritual connection, which is the main source of all of our abilities in creating the New Earth. As I have stated before, the power of the third eye was blasted open even more during the last ten years due to teachings on the law of attraction. We are now ready to take co-creation back to its true essence as we begin to connect it to our crown chakra—our spiritual connection. Spiritual co-creation is the onset of a new direction for our spiritual power. We are living in another time jump for our multisensory selves.

There has been a great shift in our psychic intuitive abilities due to our spiritual evolution. For many years as we were new to our psychic potential, we learned and played with the many abilities we were discovering. Stretching from the spiritualist movement in the 1800s to our current times, psychic potential was judged as something mysterious and magical. Some thought there was a select group that could perform such feats as mediumship, clairvoyance, and ESP.

Also, these powers were regarded with great fear as bestowed by the devil's hand. We as a global mind did not truly understand our psychic talents until great seers like Edgar Cayce emerged.

The Cayce readings helped initiate a new perception and direction for psychic power. Instead of seeing it as something to be feared or a parlor trick, we began to realize that ESP was an aspect of our soul. It was truly part of our spiritual makeup. This was a new step—to be aware that we are spiritual beings conscious of our psychic intuitive power as a healing agent for the planet. Thanks to Cayce, we were being taught an adaptable and user-friendly regimen for our inner selves, preparing us for great works for the New Golden Age.

Sadly, there is still some misperception about what psychic ability really means to our spiritual growth. Psychic power was never meant to become a wondrous accomplishment for show. But, "psychics" have become a mainstream staple in pop culture. That's fine, to a degree. Through bestselling psychic biographies, media, and television shows, people are very comfortable entertaining the notion of the psychic world in their home. But, it's jump time again. We need to eliminate the misperception of psychic celebrities and reality shows from our true spiritual practice. Psychic power should be evolving, not for show and tell, but for healing and balance.

## GETTING BEYOND THE NEED TO KNOW: PSYCHIC INTUITIVE POWER FOR THE NEW GOLDEN AGE

The progression of our spiritual power is increasingly showing us how comprehensive and authentic we are in the creation of our lives as well as in the vibrational evolution of our planet. I believe that our psychic power was never meant to be a tool for fortunetelling or side-show routines. The ego has defiantly taken hold of a very real aspect of our spiritual selves and turned it into an "entertainment only" demonstration. We have been programmed to think that people with psychic gifts have all the answers and can tell us our future. Therefore, we have become addicted "psychic-hoppers," going from one psychic to another hoping to hear what we want to hear: that our desires—mostly ego driven—will come true. Psychic power somehow lost its spiritual purpose. In my first book, *Reader of Hearts*, I state very clearly that no one should awaken to his or her spiritual path for the riches of psychic superpowers. Sadly, the lure of making money is how many current psychic celebrities market their ideas, by promising people that they can be super psychics, mediums, or healers. Here is the golden ticket; you may possess it for a price. Just as fashion magazines promote the perfect body and style, certain aspects of the fortunetelling business promote a perfect, worry-free psychic life. You are catapulted into the future with "promises" of what's around the corner.

We have become spiritual brats, spoiled by the glamour of the psychic industry that cries, "Give me, give me, and tell me my future." We have relinquished our creative potential and have given it to the chosen few who we thought were spiritual psychics. We lost our truth; we forgot that we are our own psychic consultants. Cayce educated us about this fact repeatedly. I think we are about to comprehend it, finally. We are moving into a new age of expansion concerning our spiritual abilities.

Some time ago, a friend and I were talking about the whole perception of psychic glamour and the need to reinstate its spiritual roots. My friend was just about to leave for a mediumship workshop weekend with a very well-known psychic celebrity. She had been disturbed about the conversations with other attendees via her social network. They were posting remarks such as, "I am going to be learning from the 'American Idol' of psychics, and I can't wait to become a trained medium by this person. I'll be famous!"

I was also disturbed by this discourse. There was a complete lack of conversation about the healing and spiritual aspects of this kind of work. I'm not pleased that these folks with the psychic-celebrity intentions were going to be unleashed into the public. There needs to be a shift. We should return to the true essence of psychic work, which is helping with spiritual direction and healing.

Prophecy in the Old Testament was usually focused on conveying to people the will of the Divine, the plan of destiny, and it never entertained a ridiculous question like, "Do you think that guy from the other tribe likes me?"

Enough, people! There have been a few clients who scheduled a reading with me and then become very upset when I turned the tables on them during a session instead of telling them that a handsome stranger was imminent. I would give them the psychic details about why their relationships had failed. Love yourself first. Then, the love of your life will appear. Honestly, there are many loves in our lives. The ego hates to hear that.

One lady actually screamed at me during a phone session, "I don't want to heal—I want answers!"

I responded as calmly as possible, "Then call Sylvia Browne."

"I did," she sternly answered. "I'm still waiting to see if what she said will come true."

I'm sure this client is still waiting. I don't take my sessions lightly. Most of the time, people who come to me want to heal their lives. They want to rediscover their true potential as co-creative beings. There are also those who, through lack of self-worth, spiritual intelligence, or addiction to psychic glamour, pass themselves from one willing psychic to another in a desperate attempt for the answers that will change their lives. Mind you, these answers must be authentically channeled from a powerful, all-knowing source that insists that it's not their fault that their life is chaotic.

The one thing that really hits the ego where it hurts is saying to a client, "*You are the creator of your life.*" This statement puts the full responsibility of a single soul into the vastness of her thoughts, actions, and intentions. This ownership is very powerful—but can also be very scary to the untrained soul. When one reacts harshly to the truth of spiritual responsibility, it's only because he or she is in the midst of cracking the hard-core surface of years or even lifetimes of fear-based thinking. The light is making its way back into the consciousness. Awakening is messy sometimes. Our higher self has to swim the moat of our unconsciousness to reassert its authority in the castle of our souls. Thank goodness the Divine has persistence and patience with us. Sometimes, the challenge occurs when we backslide and focus all our attention outside of ourselves. We become stuck in the signs and wonders of what's "out there."

"I need a sign, what do the tarot cards say? Can the psychic tell me what's next?" That's when we trip on the path.

We forget that all we need is within.

The metaphysical principles of the Bible warn us not to become attached to soothsayers and the like, and not because the occult was fashioned by the devil. That type of energy is not conveyed by God but by the ego. We can become highly addicted to giving our power over to someone else to tell the future. Taking ourselves away from the responsibility of our own life and giving it to another "who sees all" may sound fun and easy, but in the end, we realize that we must live and create our own lives. In order to achieve spiritual enlightenment, fully, we must move beyond the need to know our future.

I'm going to take a bold step. Let's embrace a philosophy of using psychic abilities to help evolve the planet and each other rather than to foretell the future. We are the co-creators of our future. Part of this mission of living in the New Golden Age is to proceed beyond the fear of the future and realize that we can master the power to create it. Consider whether this New Golden Age is also encouraging us to release the need for foretelling the future. Are we currently truly ready to co-create our future? Our spiritual evolution has moved us to this very awareness of our potential that the mystics from long go have been teaching us. We are there.

As I have said before, since the times of the Old Testament, our spiritual progress encompassed such a cemented perspective that seers and profits were able to read the future with precise accuracy. Since the opening of our heart chakra and the initiation of the Christ Consciousness, we have evolved to a point to where we are literally shifting our reality so fast that we are manifesting it almost immediately. Having an ideal of pure divine union like the *Christ*, we can take full responsibility in the sacred act of co-creating life with God. Seeing the future or prophesying the future has become almost obsolete.

We can see the dynamics of this change as some of our most famous living psychics have been missing the mark when it comes to foretelling future outcomes. They have in no way "lost" their gift. It's just one of the many realities showing that we, as a mass consciousness of powerful souls, are becoming more and more experienced in manipulating the present moment. Changing the present moment actually influences and alters potential future outcomes.

It is important for us to stop relying on the answers of the psychics out there. Instead, we need to look to the psychic within us in order to create our desire and destiny. We are moving even farther along our spiritual path in seeking the psychic within us to help shape and prepare for the Golden Age, which is the New Earth Consciousness. We have stepped into a new era of using our psychic powers for more universal means rather than for personal benefit. Using our intuitive powers for universal good also reshapes and, in my opinion, brings back the true role of a psychic—as a spiritual director. As I explain in my first book, *Reader of Hearts*, a psychic's true job is to bring people into the present where the soul resides and not to catapult them into the future with promises. It is the psychic's role to help people get in touch with divine wisdom—to be the channel for this wisdom without claiming to be its source.

The psychic's role is very evident in the wonderful series of books, *The Twilight Saga*. I love these books. One of the characters, Alice, is a psychic vampire. She sees the future, but it's subjective. The actual future depends upon how a person within Alice's prophetic vision chooses to react. That person might change his mind after the psychic vision has occurred. Clearly stated, someone's choice of his or her reality can and will modify the outcome of a vision. Alice's visions change whenever a person decides to do something else and proceed in a different direction. The future might always change. The unpredictability of the future is the case for authentic psychics today. Our visions are subjective due to the increased awareness of the global mind's ability to create and manipulate its own reality. This fluidity is very exciting!

To review, psychic intuitive power should always be used for its original purpose, that of spiritual direction and healing. Now that we have become more aware of our own power to co-create and to be expressions of the Divine, it's even more imperative that we progress beyond the "signs and wonders" of psychic power in order to work with its roots of spiritual well-being. When we let go of the "need to know our future," we can return to our co-creative nature. We will then take back our power and plug back into ourselves. Our spiritual self-esteem begins to magnify as we remember who we truly are. There is not one person, place, or thing outside of your spiritual self that has the power to direct you, unless you allow that to happen. In *The Wonderful Wizard of*

Oz, Glenda the Good Witch (love) warns Dorothy to stay securely inside her ruby slippers. Because of their power, the Wicked Witch of the West (fear) wanted to steal the shoes and manipulate the power for evil (misperception). This allegory is true for us. We must stay tightly tucked inside our spiritual selves, and we must never give away our power. We have had the power all along to return home—back to the source—and to make our dreams come true.

## MEDITATION TO RELEASE THE "NEED TO KNOW"

Allow yourself to relax and let go. Take a deep breath and release it. Let's take three deep breaths: one for the mind, one for the body, and one for the spirit. Let the breath that you inhale and exhale relax your entire body. Breathe deeply and easily now.

Imagine, within the middle of your being, a beautiful, golden temple of light. This temple houses your true essence, your spark of divinity. This is a safe and comfortable place to be. Allow your attention to walk into the temple, and let your mind create its interior design. On the walls you may see pictures of your close family and friends. The style of the inner dynamics of the temple is up to your imagination.

Continue to breathe deeply and easily. Don't stress, just allow your mind to create a safe place within this temple. The temple is a gift from the Divine, but how you co-create the dwelling is up to you. You are given the freedom to create whatever you want within the temple.

After a few moments, when you feel you have set the stage for your temple, look ahead to the back of the sacred dwelling. There you will see an empty altar. You are now given free access to create your altar. You may see pictures of important master teachers, guides, and other beings who have brought you great wisdom and joy. You are still breathing deeply and easily. Don't forget to create some light for your altar, as you may see candles appear at this time. Incense, with its soft smoky perfume, manifests to raise the vibration of your altar. What's your favorite scent? Allow the mind to create it. See it. Smell it. Experience it. You can actually inhale the scent, taking a deep, full, cleansing breath. Allow the sacred scent to cleanse you.

As you stand within your temple, realize that this is your home. Your true place of residence is within. Nothing can harm you here, and nothing can take this sacred place away from you. All of your co-creative talent emanates from this place. All of your worries and challenges are also brought here, to surrender. You surrender your problems and let them wash away.

See the vibrant light arising from your temple, surrounding you and enveloping you. The light is your psychic intuitive power. It is a part of you, and it expands outward into your daily life. It gives you navigation and direction. Your intuition stays the course on the right and true path for you.

You have no need to fear the future because here, in this sacred place, you create it. With the hand of God reminding you to hold your personal power tightly around you, you are able to live in the present. The Divine moves through you, directing along with you the next step in your life. Every step is faith-filled, and an inner knowing keeps you focused on the beautiful lesson of co-creation.

Letting go of the need to know is very liberating. Within this sacred inner temple, you have filled yourself with the consciousness of divine reassurance that all will be well, and that you will be guided and navigated through any life challenge. All the worries of tomorrow and yesterday fade away. All you have today and every day is the present moment with God.

With this embodiment of God's light shining from your inner temple, you can be a beacon of healing and guidance not only for yourself but also for others. Light attracts light. You are now a guidepost, a living example of the power and presence of divinity. You consistently open to your psychic intuitive power with the intention to heal, to balance, and to restore. Healing or helping is the purpose behind all of your spiritual talents.

Take a deep breath and allow this renewed awareness to saturate your mind, body, and emotions. Let it be one with you. Now bring your attention back to the room. Allow your inner temple of light to reside within you—safe and secure. You can return anytime you want. Permit yourself to come back to consciousness, still breathing deeply and easily. Take this energy out into your daily life, and let it be your inner compass for co-creation.

# 3 The Holy Spirit: The Sacred Embodiment of the Divine Feminine

*I*n the spiritual healing aspect of my work, I have found that the foundation for everything I do and teach is built on guidance from and awareness of the Holy Spirit. It's imperative in the co-creative process concerning the Golden Age of Enlightenment for the conscious soul to become intimate and mindful of the presence of God's breath of life, the Holy Spirit. Growing up in the South and being raised as a Baptist, the Holy Spirit was often preached about but was never actually explained. Over many years of studying mystical Christianity and other such ancient texts, I began to figure out why there was such a cloak of mystery around the third aspect of the Holy Triad. It represents not so much a mystery but rather a deliberate edict of the liberating force of God's true nature. In my youth, I would hear the discussions of my uncles and cousins—all ministers or deacons—about being blessed by the Holy Spirit or being washed in the salvation of the Holy Spirit. The only idea I could gather from their "oh so wise teachings" (sarcasm there), was that this Holy Spirit was some sort of connection between God and Jesus and was also our ticket out of the fiery depths of hell. My intuition felt that something was amiss. Luckily, my inquisitive and open mind began to investigate other sources, and that's where I discovered a great confirmation and realization of who the Holy Spirit truly was.

## WHO IS THE HOLY SPIRIT?

The Holy Spirit is the living breath of the Mother/Father God. She is the anointer of wisdom, grace, spiritual awakening, and Pure Divine Love. The word holy means "whole" and spirit is equivalent to "being." So the Holy Spirit can be thought of as a force pushing all existence toward wholeness. When this energy is called, it helps sustain balance and restore peace, bringing wholeness back to an individual or a situation. The Edgar Cayce readings also identified the Holy Spirit as the "motivating force" for the union of God and man. In the early Christian and Hebrew texts, this divine presence was often referred to as *Shekinah* or *Sophia*, the goddess of wisdom. *Shekinah* is translated as a word for the divine feminine from ancient Hebrew, literally meaning the "dwelling place of God." In sacred temples throughout the early Judeo Christian texts, this divine presence was described as clouds of smoke that manifested during sacred rituals. Moses was communicated with by the "*Shekinah*" via the burning bush. So in essence, the spirit of God connected to mankind and created "dwelling places" for the union of the physical and spiritual being.

While teaching at my public events, at what I call healing sanctuaries, I invoke the power of the Holy Spirit. This invocation is not so much a calling of something outside of me to appear, but rather a calling forth of spiritual power from within, to well up within the hearts of all those attending the service. The liberating power of God is the purifier of all ills. Whether it's a physical, mental, emotional, or even a spiritual disaster within the body, the Holy Spirit's intent when it's awakened within is to correct our thoughts and bring us back into alignment with God. The Holy Spirit literally creates a sacred dwelling place within us, forming an energetic temple of the living God. The manifestation of the Holy Spirit is the most extraordinary and fulfilling aspect of my work. When I witness my students and clients finally discover the power within themselves, it's a true miracle. The Holy Spirit was sent to us as a gift of salvation.

The Holy Spirit has been sent not in the sense of God's saying, "Believe my way," but rather in the sense of a guiding force that is helping us remember our true nature as children of the most high. When the master, Jesus, was baptized by St. John the Baptist, that sacred ritual was initiated by the Holy Spirit as a pervasive fixture in our spiritual natures. After the baptism, the Holy Spirit intensified in Jesus, and he became the Christ (Pure Enlightenment), symbolically giving us a pattern for which we can also be baptized. All we have to do is to call forth her everlasting power of liberation as we remember our divinity.

There is a misperception, especially in fundamental Christianity, of the true nature and purpose of the Holy Spirit. Unfortunately, the spirit of God is "invoked" to encourage the masses to believe in whatever particular dogma is being preached at the moment. This manipulation is not the work of the Holy Spirit. It is the work of fear. The Holy Spirit's function has always been to bring wholeness and union back to the consciousness of a person—not to control a belief system. This universal energy has no particular religion or belief system that "owns" it. It is the creative and healing force of God that no man "owns" but is blessed with, instead. There are many names for the Holy Spirit, and I'm sure many of you are familiar with such terms as life force, prana, and chi. Putting the Spirit of God into a box is a lost cause.

Let me give you an example of the role of the Holy Spirit in your life. Think of yourself as a mobile phone. The Holy Spirit is the "satellite" within the universe that beams information, downloads, and upgrades into your system, and the Christ Consciousness is your ideal mobile plan that has the best connection, minutes, and worldwide coverage. All of this is available at no cost. Therefore, the Holy Spirit is the direct link to the source of all creation, giving you the opportunity to live in the well-being of God's divine plan. The Holy Spirit helps to shift your thoughts to the ideal of the Christ Consciousness, which is true enlightenment.

The reason the Holy Spirit has been viewed as feminine in nature resides in the fact that its essence is that of a comforter, healer, and counselor. Just as a loving mother provides a child with comfort, help, and guidance, so operates the Holy Spirit in your life. You can see why power-hungry religions might try to hide her true nature from the

masses. If you give power to the people and show them how connected
they are to God on their own merit, there might be no need for a religion at all. Personal communication with the Holy Spirit is very liberating. The time has come for the institutions founded by external power
and egocentric religious attitudes to step aside, for a true revival of the
Holy Spirit is upon us. We are awakening to her life–giving miracles
because we know she resides within us. We can call on her guidance at
any time.

I want to give you some steps for opening up to the Holy Spirit's
presence in your life. From that awakening, you can build the strongest
spiritual foundation you have ever had. With the New Golden Age vibrating all around us, a spiritual foundation built firmly on Divine Love
is necessary.

## BUILDING A SPIRITUAL FOUNDATION

The most important thing to remember during the New Golden Age
is to sustain your spiritual foundation. Everything depends on that un-
derpinning. Your career, relationships, and health all rest on the power
built by your spiritual foundation. Learning how the Holy Spirit works
with you concerning guiding your life direction and correcting your
thoughts can help you achieve well–being in all areas of your life. Below are what I call gifts and fruits of the spirit that I have found in my
own life as well as in my clients' lives. The gifts and fruits of the Holy
Spirit become active in anyone who opens to her presence.

Each gift can help you co–create a strong and healthy life, within as
well as without. Much has been written about these gifts and the quan-
tity of these gifts of the spirit. I have reduced them to an essential four
that I have seen in my collaborating with the Holy Spirit as the most
prominent. I want you to think of a gift as the awareness and of the fruit
as the nourishment of that awareness, in reference to the list below.

A Course in Miracles teaches that we can ask the Holy Spirit to correct
our thinking and help us to switch our thoughts from fear to love. In
turn, the four gifts and fruits listed below become activated truth in our
psyche, giving us the spiritual power to live as God intended, surrounded by well–being and love. If you also regard these gifts as part of

your psychic intuitive nature, it will give an even deeper meaning to all of our hunches and inner knowing as reliable guidance from the Holy Spirit. I have added a short prayer with each of the four gifts and fruits to help you activate them within your own inner landscape. For an even greater connection, I have included an invocation of the Holy Spirit in "The Invocations" chapter of this book.

## THE FOUR GIFTS AND FRUITS OF THE HOLY SPIRIT: A PSYCHIC PERSPECTIVE

### Gift: Clarity, Fruit: Faith

The Holy Spirit is able to clear away all mental confusion and allow our divine eyes to see the reality of our life. From fear to love, our ability see circumstances and relationships clearly and with no attachment reinforces our power to navigate through life's challenges. From this renewed sense of clear direction, our faith in the Divine and ourselves is in turn reinstated to deal with our challenges head-on and with spiritual clarity. From a clear space activated by the Holy Spirit within, we can make better choices based on love. Reacting from fear causes even more confusion.

> Come, Holy Spirit. You are the provider of clarity and truth. Open my eyes to your light so that it may brighten my path. From your light, all illusion fades, and I see clearly with divine eyes. I choose love, and your presence embraces me with peace. Amen.

### Gift: Courage, Fruit: Patience

The Holy Spirit gives us the courage to carry on. We have heard of people who have been raised up in the spirit. This is the awareness that with God, anything is possible, even when all hope seems lost. One prayer for strength from a willing soul can change the world. From courage, we receive the power of patience. Patience allows our courage to build and strengthen. Patience also allows the universe to give us all its glory without need of control. "Not my will but thine" is the most powerful step in the journey of spiritual awakening. We are strong in the spirit, and it moves us beyond all boundaries of fear and sadness.

> Come, Holy Spirit. Fill my heart with your courage and valor.
> I know that when I raise my spiritual sword, it will cut
> through any and all ties that hold me away from your light.
> Spirit of the living God, I rest in the assurance that all is well
> in my world and that your holy grace never falters and never
> fails. Amen.

## Gift: Discernment, Fruit: Awareness

One of the most essential tools for one's spiritual path is discernment. The Holy Spirit is the translator of all information that we receive on a daily basis. Those "red flags" that we see when we know something is not in sync or right for us are gifts of discernment at work. The awareness of our truth builds in our spiritual system increasingly as we listen and do what feels right to us. The Holy Spirit also helps us to truly see behind the mask and the lies, whether they are ours or someone else's. When we live in truth, we recognize its presence. We also recognize when its presence is lacking in ourselves and in others. This is the gift of discernment, seeing illusion for what it is and reclaiming our truth.

> Come, Holy Spirit. Shower me with your everlasting light. I
> open my heart and mind to your divine care and love. I see
> everything in my life with open eyes and an open heart. All
> illusion and darkness fall away, and the road to truth is clear.
> With your hand, you guide me safely through the trials of
> fear and falsehood and liberate my soul to understand what's
> true for me. Amen.

## Gift: Healing, Fruit: Balance

All of the gifts and fruits point to the main role of the Holy Spirit's intentions: healing. Healing is the balance of mind, body, emotion, and soul in union with God. Remember that the Holy Spirit is pushing all existence toward wholeness. Any and all dis-ease in our minds and bodies can become whole again by way of the Holy Spirit's manifestation. From this manifestation within, we heal by remembering our divine connection as children of the most high. Only by forgetfulness of our true nature do we cause separateness and dis–ease.

> Come, Holy Spirit. Lift my heart, my mind, my body, and my soul to your very presence; I'm enveloped in a cocoon of your healing and wholeness. Every cell, every organ, and every bone of my body is washed clean by your waters of well-being. I accept your healing today and every day. From your healing, I remember. I remember that I am a child of the most high. Amen.

## FINAL THOUGHTS ON THE HOLY SPIRIT

From these four powerful gifts and fruits of the spirit, you can realize how essential working with the Holy Spirit is to enhance your role as minister and helper in the New Golden Age of Enlightenment. With the Holy Spirit's help, you can go directly to the source of all creation. Cut out the middleman, I always say; and heal, teach, and co–create directly with the pure essence of God.

One important thing to remember while working with the Holy Spirit is that you are not dealing with a force outside of you. The Holy Spirit is part of your spiritual makeup. When it's called, it wells up from within you. Using our example of a satellite, when you have a bad connection and you are immersed in thoughts of fear, you tend to "drop calls" from the Holy Spirit's guidance. If we remember to shift our thoughts from fear to love by asking for her guidance, we will once again sustain our true spiritual connection and receive clear communication.

As a child of God awakened to spiritual power, you are always the source for healing and well-being. The Holy Spirit is within you and ready to be of service in the reinstatement of your faith and liberation from fear.

When I give my healing services, I'm often asked about angels and spirit guides in respect to the Holy Spirit. Here are my thoughts about angels, spirit guides, and the Holy Spirit. I feel that the Holy Spirit will manifest in many forms in your life—in whatever form you are comfortable with during a particular stage of your spiritual growth. These manifestations are what I call the divine archetypes. I write in depth on this topic in the chapter about spiritual deliverance. At some point, though, one must be ready to work directly with God; and to me, that's communicating with the Holy Spirit. Angels and guides are a type of personnel of the Holy Spirit and are always under her direction regarding your spiritual path. No matter what name or face you give it, everything happens by the grace of God. Angels, guides, and the Holy Spirit are all manifestations of your personal spiritual power.

For further study of the Holy Spirit, see the Resources list at the end of this book.

## MEDITATION TO RELEASE THE POWER OF THE HOLY SPIRIT

Come, Holy Spirit; fill my heart with your healing vibration and light. Teach me the truth of my co-creative power, and educate me in my role as a Master of Light. I am a divine child of God. I am a perfect embodiment of health. I am a master of your sacred energy, Holy Spirit. Thank you. Thank you for your presence as my teacher, my healer, and my guide. Keep me ever in your embrace, and let me show the world your brilliance just by being an example—conscious of being charity, truth, and love. I am here, Holy Spirit, come. Come into my life, well up from within my very being, never to leave. You are my home. Amen.

# 4 Anchor the Light: The Work of Spiritual Deliverance

hrough information received from my psychic source, clients, and students, there is an upwelling of something that I'm sure most of you have experienced during this great quickening of consciousness. I've witnessed the fact that many people are losing their mental health to a degree, with some even checking out of their bodies in the process. There is a sense of a spiritual psychosis around us. People are literally flipping out. Why is this happening? My "psychic sources" have asked me to convey some important information to you. I will have to reveal another aspect of my work that I usually do not disclose, but when "Source" directs me to educate and inform the masses, I comply.

First, it's very clear that we are on the fast track of spiritual awakening right now. Everybody's "stuff" is surfacing. Like it or not, the gods are demanding that we get all of our ducks in a row relative to our inner dynamics. Since 2009, we have been somewhat lazy regarding our inner progression. Not all of us, mind you, have been lazy with our spirituality. There has been a perception that when 2012 arrives, "we will all be okay," and maybe we won't have to work so hard. That is not true! When 2012 rolled in, we crossed a spiritual barrier into a faster and more progressive inner awakening. Even those who think they are the "bee's knees" when it comes to enlightenment are being shown otherwise. There is always more to learn about and expand upon when it comes to our inner selves. Truth and authentic revelations for each soul on this planet now comprise a Pandora's box. There is no time to view your spiritual life as a hobby. It must be a lifestyle and a daily practice. 2012's consciousness was the catalyst to release all that prevents each soul from fully experiencing and embodying God's divine light. How can we initiate the "New Earth" if we still have places within ourselves that are bound by an inner darkness or our shadow selves?

So here is where I tell you that the foundation of most of my work is spiritual deliverance, better known to some as exorcism. As you read this statement, I know that many of you are thinking of demonic children who spit out pea soup and curse freely. That vision might be entertaining but is not very accurate. My work in this area includes helping individuals, alive or dead. We release and balance the negative energy possessing their soul or auric bodies to allow the light of higher consciousness (the Holy Spirit) to permeate them. It's not unlike changing your thoughts from negative to positive, but the scale is more dynamic. When a soul has such a dramatic shift in its awakening process, many years of dark, unconscious energy may rise to the surface. The great psychologist, Carl Jung, called this aspect of the unconscious our shadow self. The shadow, or "shadow aspect," is a part of the *unconscious mind* consisting of *repressed*, fear-based thoughts and belief systems. Everyone embodies a shadow self. Native American cultures called it "our trickster." In the Christian religion, the shadow was labeled as Satan. I want to assert that we are not talking about, in this case, a personalized evil being. I'll address that topic later in this chapter. We are talking about a self-induced process of negativity or unconsciousness—*A Course in Miracles* would call this the ego. Don't believe the myth that this unconsciousness is something you can blame, as if to say, "The devil made me do it!" By talking about spiritual deliverance in this chapter, I'm delving deeply into the darkest parts of our psyche and soul to help you see how powerful you really are. To embody God's everlasting light, you must first perceive the darkness that blocks you from receiving it fully.

Jung goes on to convey in his works that the shadow, instinctive and *irrational in nature*, is prone to *projection*. The shadow projects or changes its personal inferiority into a perceived moral deficiency in someone else. Jung indicates that if these projections are unrecognized, the projection-making factor (the shadow self) then has a free hand and can realize its object. These projections insulate and cripple individuals by forming an ever-thicker fog of illusion between the ego and the real world. In my work with spiritual deliverance, I find Jung's assessment of this "shadow aspect" to be accurate. You can read more about the parts of ourselves in Chapter 6 of *The Portable Jung*, edited by Joseph Campbell. People might become possessed by their own darkness if it is not resolved. These dark thoughts and emotions may become a type of intelligence all its own, over time. When you focus your thoughts and emotions solely on fear, hate, anger, rage, and sadness, they build into what I call "chaos elementals." A challenging fact is that not only living people are susceptible to this shadow possession and projection. Lost souls or ghosts wander in this chaos and are stuck in it. The place where they are trapped in limbo is called the "Outer Darkness," or some would call it Hell. This entrapment is why it's so important for lost souls to be guided to the light. They, too, can release their own binding darkness and finally be free. Think of it this way: when you are in a bad mood, it can cloud your day, and you are left feeling deflated. A lost soul has this same challenge, but it's magnified tenfold. The souls are pure energy, and the magnification of fear is even more prominent in them. Think how blessed we are (in the form of our body) to be able to call up a friend or to consult a therapist. Where do lost souls get counsel when they are so clouded by their own chaos elementals that they can't see the angelic helpers trying to guide them home? I'm getting ahead of myself here, but you probably understand my point.

Ron Roth, PhD, a spiritual healer, bestselling author, and teacher, was a dear friend and mentor of mine for many years. He has long passed from his physical body, but his teachings and spirit live on. He explained what chaos elementals, or elementals, are in his book, *Prayer and the Five Stages of Healing*, on page 80:

**The early mystics believed that one could be possessed by**

negative spiritual energy by one's own device, which they called "Elementals." We can produce these thought-forms or elementals subconsciously or consciously, and though we project them outward they eventually return to our own subconscious. [What you project, you get back!] The more we create and project these negative elementals, the more sustenance they take from our own unconscious, until they possess us. Human beings who have died but who, because of their negative energies, remain stuck on the earth plane can besiege us with those energies. Whether negative thoughts, desires, and feelings come from within us or are induced in us by restless departed souls, they can cause our energy field to vibrate at certain frequencies, which in turn determine the type and quality of elementals (thought-forms) we create. We must learn to create elementals of love that will dissolve the negative elementals, no matter where they come from. Just as we are always surrounded by God's grace, which is available to us if we learn to tune into it through prayer, [inner attunement] we are also surrounded by environmental thought energies and [entities] that are less than positive. If we open ourselves to these energies with our negative thoughts and attitudes, they can assume a life of their own and possess us in somewhat the same way that a bad habit possesses us.

Ron Roth could not have explained it more plainly. It is of the utmost importance that we intercept our negative thoughts, live in Divine Love, and make Love our foundation for a healthy lifestyle. I see many people who have no spiritual foundation who are nevertheless awakening and shifting, resulting in the projection of much unconscious and negative energy. Just as there are great amounts of spiritual activity occurring on our side of reality, there is just as much happening in the spirit realms, as well. We must learn to stay grounded and balanced during the holy quickening of our planet so that our transition into the New Golden Age of Enlightenment will be initiated with as much ease as possible.

I'd like to take you into a more in-depth explanation of spiritual deliverance work or the "sacred rite of exorcism." First let me step onto a soapbox. There are many in the dogmatic religious and fundamentalist communities who practice spiritual deliverance work or the sacred rite of exorcism to manipulate the masses with their own control- and fear-based belief systems. Those who mock this sacred rite or try to use it with unfavorable intentions will fail to heal or free anyone. They are just reinstating an obsessive, fear-based psychosis in their victims. The true essence of the rite of exorcism or spiritual deliverance work is the removal of fear so that Divine Love can prevail, purely and simply. Then that soul—in body or out of body—is free to live and prosper in the Light of the Divine in whatever way it sees fit. The Master Jesus *never* healed or exorcised anyone by first asking what he or she believed. He did not demand that anyone believe in a certain way in order to be set free. *Rubbish!* He laid hands on anyone who asked or on anyone to whom the Holy Spirit directed him. His intention was to awaken the living breath of God within and open the afflicted ones' hearts to the truth that they were indeed the children of the most high.

All people who are gay, straight, black, white, religious, pagan or whatever the nationality, sexuality, or spirituality are open to receive the blessing of deliverance to enhance their uniqueness ordained by God. This work is *not* intended to make anyone change to fit the "exorcist's" personal, religious, or political beliefs. Its sole purpose is to liberate the Living Breath of God and reestablish the foundation of Divine Love. This reinstatement allows the people who are being delivered to embrace their lives and become the perfect being God intended them to be. If you're gay, you are going to be a healthy gay person who loves himself as God does. If you are a pagan, then you will be the best earth-loving pagan you can be. I hope I have made myself very clear.

As I explained earlier, "chaos elementals" are derived from our own obsessive thoughts. If they are not properly addressed, those thoughts can and will become a type of concentrated negative energy that will affect our spiritual energy bodies. I refer again to Master Ron Roth's book, *Prayer and the Five Stages of Healing*. Roth states that these negative spiritual energies [or chaos elementals] do not inhabit the body so much as they reside in the energy fields surrounding the body. They gain access to us through various phobias, addictions, or confused psychological states. Christian mystics referred to our fears, addictions, and phobias as access points or open doors by which these negative energies might possess us. One reason why this phenomenon occurs is that strong feelings of separation, alienation, and abandonment will manifest when people go through their own "dark night of the soul" or spiritual shifting. When you shift from the life that you thought was real into the true reality of spiritual awakening, the growing pains might be harsh. Feelings of fear and separation act as magnets for negative energies in the atmosphere.

The task is to move through the shift while building a strong spiritual foundation of union with God and avoiding the feeling of separation. Don't stay in the muck or you'll sink! We all desire to reunite with the Divine. Continue to walk forward, and God will always meet you halfway.

The dark night of the soul, or what I like to call it—divine darkness—is an aspect of our spiritual growth that asks us to purify and balance our inner selves. When we first awaken to the reality of our spiritual lives, there is a type of inner housekeeping that must be processed. The divine darkness stage of our spiritual awakening initiates an essential energy detox. It causes a breakdown in your emotional, mental, and physical life that disrupts all of your old patterns. It helps you release your attachment to people, places, and things that no longer serve your higher good and that are not healthy for you. During this process, we might observe a considerable amount of negativity being released. It's not unlike the example of pouring fresh water into a vase that has collected dirt and twigs in its base—the waters rush in and the debris floods out.

During our own dark nights, we intuitively open up our ideas. Our psychic nature becomes more magnified due to the spiritual upwelling from our inner selves. During this spiritual cleansing, we are not only dealing with the manifestation of self-induced negativity, but we may also be affected by the negativity of lost souls who are consumed by their own unconsciousness. Again, when we open up to spirit, we become more sensitive to energies within us and all around us. I remember when I began to experience this awakening as a young teenager. At this time, I did not realize what was happening. I began seeing energy and lights dancing around individuals whom I encountered. While growing up, it seemed like someone had turned on the "vacancy sign" in my bedroom: spirits visited in and out frequently. Remember, when we begin to shine our light from within, we are like moths to a flame for those who are living or dead. They want what we have, because they have not yet found their own inner light. I can't stress enough why our inner awakening and spiritual self–reliance are so important. Just as we keep our physical immune system healthy, we should do the same for our spiritual immunity.

My intention for this chapter is not to frighten you but to strengthen you. I'm not talking about this type of spiritual dynamic to introduce a sense of paranormal spookiness. Instead, I want to reinforce how powerful you are and emphasize the importance of maintaining your spiritual stamina during this time of global awakening. The fact remains that the more love you infuse in your life through thought and action, the less you will come into contact with lower vibrational entities or energies. It is that simple. I have been somewhat hesitant to describe this type of work because some fearful people tend to become paranoid, seeing demons around every corner. Please trust me when I write that the hefty negativity of a demon is very rarely encountered. I don't care what the reality shows portray on television. Always return to a grounded perspective in this work, knowing that the ultimate truth is that we must always confront our own inner demons and dissolve them with our heightened states of Divine Love. If we don't use our spiritual power to balance our lives, then we are susceptible to our own inner chaos as well as the energies of chaos that are attracted to our dysfunctions. Remember that like attracts like. Keep it light, people! The purpose of our spiritual awakening and dark nights is to realize the power of our thoughts. We learn how to shift fear into love with just one switch of the mind. Often, we create many of these impersonal negative energies, elementals, or thought–forms ourselves. They can and do affect our spiritual development. We need to become aware of the presence of, and how we generate, these negative energies so that we can take steps to inhibit their activity.

# INVOKING THE SACRED FOR SPIRITUAL
# CLEANSING AND PROTECTION

How do you keep your energy high, banishing any negative energy that might be affecting you? The first line of defense is learning to keep your thoughts and emotions in check. Always do your best to catch your thoughts when they are directed by fear. Notice them, and re-think them into more loving perspectives. You are always the director of how you think and perceive the world. Thoughts are truly things, as you have read so far. The purpose of this entire book and its teachings is to support you as you rebuild and reinforce your strong, inner land-scape where only love resides. Second, build your meditation and prayer life into a daily practice. The more you exercise your spiritual bodies with love, the stronger they become. Know that by living your life from the spiritual power within, you are always protected and blessed by the light and presence of the Divine. It's only in the forgetting of our divine natures that we open a door to our own self-induced negativity. It's only in the prolonging of our unconscious reality by the choices we make that we digress even further to invite outside negativity, as well. Fear and Love always rest on your power of choice.

I have always found prayer and invocation to be the best remedy for switching gears from fear to love. When you are feeling low in energy and not in harmony with your spirit, a simple affirmative prayer may open your mind and heart to catch the thoughts of God. When you are having a disappointing day and thinking loving thoughts seems to be a chore, just ask the Holy Spirit to help you open to her presence. Here is a lovely, prayerful affirmation that I like to use during those frustrating moments:

> Divine Love, be in my thoughts. Divine Love, be in my words. Divine Love, be in my actions—today and every day. I am Divine Love.

See? It's simple. A few words with the intent of Divine Love behind them can change everything. We can take our power back by not react-ing to people who indulge in their own self-pity or negativity. We can walk away from them or maintain our spiritual armor so that we are not affected by anything they say. We are powerful. There is great truth in the affirmation from the Unity Church: "Nothing disturbs the calm peace of my soul." The more we hold tightly to that thought, the less we will draw to us any negative energy. "As within so without," the ancients wisely stated.

Even though you are maintaining the strength of your inner dynamics, you may still come into contact with other energetic entities that may not be so conscious of their own spiritual power. We live in a world that is inhabited by both the living and the dead. There are all sorts of energies—within and outside of the body—residing on this planet. Some of them are peaceful beings and some are not as peaceful. Similarly, in everyday life for the living, there are wonderful people and there are also scoundrels. The first thing to remember on the slim chance that you encounter negativity in the energetic form is that *you are a child of the Mother/Father God.* Nothing can harm you when you are standing strong in that truth. You have the *divine power* to dispel negativity and banish it from your personal energy, home, and family. I refer you to the invocations in Chapter 9 to use as needed.

Prayer and invocations are your most powerful tools against negativity, self-induced or otherwise. Invoking the power of God has been used for centuries to ward off evil, with good reason. It works! In this period of the great Shift, it is time to truly learn how to use our spiritual power in the variety of ways that are available to us. I don't want you to think that you are using some sort of magic spell. You are not calling these spiritual powers from outside of you when you are invoking sacred energy. You are actually calling forth the spiritual powers from within you. The more spiritual self-esteem you have within, the more powerful your prayers will become.

If you are praying without the awareness that you are a child of God, the negativity will magnify your sense of separateness from the Divine. Again, we build strong spiritual foundations in our lives in order to stand firmly in the awareness that we are *God's* within. For example, if you say an affirmation for abundance while you still feel and believe in scarcity, it will cancel itself out. I'm not saying that God won't come to your aid; your spiritual resources always do. But if fear is the prominent emotion, then you are giving authority to fear more than to love. If that's the case, then fear will always play with you like a puppet on a string. You can't serve two masters. The choice is yours. Marianne Williamson explained that when you build your house on sand (fear), it will wash away. When you build your house on rock (love), it will stand.

## THE DIVINE ARCHETYPES

There is an array of spiritual resources within us, which we can invoke in times of distress. We can also call upon these resources when we need some extra energy once in a while. Whatever you want to call these resources—angels or guides—these energy resources are manifested from within our own spiritual power. That's why I prefer to call these helpful and protective energies divine archetypes. Archetypes are energetic patterns of influence that are ancient, mystical, and universally shared, such as mother, father, victim, queen, or hero. As visual symbols or energetic imprints, archetypes are forever present within our psyches. I'm introducing a new perspective with my idea of the divine archetype as a spiritual energy. I have encountered these energies many times during psychic readings with clients, and also in my own life.

The first time I consciously encountered a divine archetypal energy was while I was on a speaking tour in the Deep South. I was doing a reading for a woman in a lovely little city called Lafayette, Louisiana. I was psychically tapping into her energy, when I suddenly saw within my mind's eye St. Joan of Arc, standing right beside her. I realized that a very powerful energy had just taken up residence. I told the woman that Joan of Arc was manifest and standing next to her. The lady began to tear up and revealed that she had been praying to Saint Joan for strength during her ordeal with a bad relationship. The energy that comprised Joan of Arc said nothing but was present as a type of security blanket for my client, a type of spiritual reinforcement. The woman went on to affirm that Joan of Arc was her favorite saint. Let me explain that this part of Louisiana where I was on tour is heavily steeped in Catholicism. The saints, therefore, were very popular as archetypal forces within the local psyche of this particular community. After the session,

I asked my own inner guidance about the powerful energy that manifested during the readings: was it the actual spirit of Joan of Arc? My source relayed that this energy could be described as a divine archetype of Joan of Arc. As it was not the actual soul of Joan, it was nevertheless an archetypal symbol of power and strength that my client had called up from her own spiritual resources within.

This force manifested as St. Joan of Arc to support my client's' familiarity and perception of a powerful being. I loved this information and recognized it as another level of understanding in our relationship to the Divine. I had never heard of this kind of information before. Many people routinely called to St. Michael or Mother Mary as if they were spiritual powers outside of themselves. I did not always accept this idea. I believe strongly that people should accept their own divine power without relying on something outside of themselves. The information gleaned from this reading made perfect sense. We invoke a divine archetype, and the symbolic energy becomes a means of power and wisdom from within our own psyche and spiritual consciousness. These divine archetypes are within us!

This belief reestablishes our strength from within. It also confirms my intuitive feeling that we are all worthy of the power of God. We obtain it from our inner resources. In fact, we are even more connected to the Divine when we realize that asking for guidance from saints, angels, or spirit guides is not something that will be answered from outside of ourselves. Instead, their archetypal aid is manifested from within our own consciousness. It is then projected outward and remedied. We are holding on to our own powerful natures without identifying our responsibility in life situations as "something" outside of ourselves. Perceiving our relationship in this way with these spiritual defenders and guardians as archetypal forces reinforces our own inner union with God. It does not separate us when we believe that these beings are no better or stronger than we are. They are just like us because they are filtered through our own spiritual resources. In truth, we are one with God and all creation.

For example, think of your favorite hero or movie star when you were a child. The powerful attributes that you loved in that person are the very attributes you carry within yourself. We must have the same talents and potential in ourselves or we would never recognize the same reflection in anyone else. This idea is true regarding all the saints, masters, and spiritual gurus to whom we are attracted. The sacredness of the Divine that these people manifested while living in their bodies is reflected within us. If you are drawn to the Archangel Michael, then you carry the same powerful aspects of strength and valor within yourself. If it's Saint Francis you admire, then you are bestowed with the same respect and affinity for nature as he embodied. Do you see? Just as a really good actor assumes a role, he or she invokes the archetypal force of the character and becomes that character. In understanding divine archetypes, the very same principle is employed. When you pray or call to a sacred force, you become an embodiment of it.

Let's refer to the power of choice to be influenced by negative or positive energy. Either way you choose to use energetic power, it can and will uplift you or bring you down by your own intention. The desirability of positive energy is the reason to work with love, and the divine archetypes will help us sustain a strong spiritual foundation.

As with the nature and balance of the universe, with the light comes the dark. I want to tell you a story about spiritual deliverance and the release of what I call dark archetypes. This chapter has gone into detail about chaos elementals and how we can be possessed by negative thoughts. The following story reveals by pure intention what happens when one invokes dark archetypes. There are consequences for "playing" in the dark.

## DARRIN THE VAMPIRE SLAYER!?

Many years ago I worked for a large, retail bookstore. One night after work, I decided to spend some time with friends while enjoying coffee lattes. We were seated out on the storefront patio. As we sipped our coffee, we all agreed that a hot drink was a bad idea. It was a humid summer night, and the air seemed thick with perspiration. At this point, I had remained fairly quiet about my psychic life, continuing to study on my own. I had given a few readings here and there. Not popularized yet, I was still a rookie psychic, or so I thought. As we chatted, my attention was broken when I noticed a tall young man with blazing red bushy hair, dressed in black, walking into the front of the bookstore. I noticed him because he seemed determined about something, and I felt a strange twist in my stomach. I knew that the strange energy emanated from him.

When I turned my attention back to my group, I noticed that they had embarked on a political conversation. I opted out of the discussion and closed my eyes while sipping slowly from my latte. My eyes had been closed for just a few seconds when I felt an immense amount of heat and heaviness next to me. This time, I knew that it was not the humidity. I looked up and was startled to see that the red-haired young man whom I had seen earlier was now standing right next to me. I spit my latte all over myself with a gasp. I looked over at my friends, but they were oblivious to anything else as they continued their discussion regarding the merits of Republicans versus the Democrats.

I looked up again and saw that this young man was almost in tears. He gazed down at me with hopeless, dark brown—almost black—eyes.

"Can I help you?" I said.

"Yes," he answered sternly. "They say you can help me." He looked like he was frozen in his tracks and unable to move.

I got up. "Oh, okay, do you need help with finding a book? I'm off the clock, but I will help you find something."

"No," he exclaimed, "*they said you can help me!*" His voice rose to a deep, guttural kind of sound.

Oh, great, I thought. *They?* I looked over and noticed that my friends were still in their own little world and paying no attention to the two of us. I had a feeling that this request was not about locating a book and that it was about to become very interesting. I led him over to an empty corner of the patio. He could barely walk and became sweaty and shaky.

"Help me, please!" He whispered.

"Okay," I said. I began receiving psychic impressions from him. I saw massive amounts of darkness and negative thought-forms covering him completely. His energy looked like that of a plague victim. I knew he had opened himself up to it and was playing around with dark magic. He had opened a window and a "big bad entity" had entered. I saw cuts and teeth marks on his wrist. "You're into vampirism," I stated.

He looked up and held out his arms. "Yes," he said.

I saw images of him as he was initiated into a vampire cult. He truly did not realize what he had summoned. But, he wanted power, and this kind of energy was his way to get it. The dark archetype of the vampire was invoked, plus some other elements that I don't want to describe here. The images flooded through my mind like a movie. I could see that his life had been a rough one. Being abandoned by his father and having had a drug-addicted mother had been challenging. His life review showed me the many reasons why this soul had stepped off the path. I was snapped back into the present moment as the young man's voice commanded my attention again.

"The voices said you can help me. I want out. I want to be free." His voice was shaky; he could barely utter the words.

Whatever energy he had invoked did not want to let him go. Because of his desire to change and his prayer for help, divine guidance pierced the darkness and delivered him to my doorstep—surprise, surprise.

Oh, my God, I thought. I have never encountered anything like this situation before. Even now, no one was looking our way. It seemed as though we were in an invisible bubble. At this point, my whole body was vibrating, and I jumped into "slayer," mode, I guess. I looked him in the eye: "Will you open yourself for a prayer of release and purification?"

"Yes," he said.

"Are you willing to let this energy go?" I asked.

"Yes," he said, but I could see that it was getting harder for him to speak. Mercy, what if he starts spitting out pea soup, I thought with apprehension.

I laid my hand on his forehead; the Catholics do it this way, I thought. I began to invoke the Holy Spirit. "Come, Holy Spirit," I proclaimed loudly.

He fell to his knees.

"Come, Holy Spirit and banish this negativity away, through the power of the Christ Consciousness." I then called for the protective guidance of the Archangel Michael, another strong divine archetype, to help banish this bad entity. I thought the kid was going into convulsions. I continued on and on with the invocations. He was still on his knees when he suddenly stopped shaking. I could feel the heaviness of his energy clear up and lighten. I was glad he did not scream, curse, or vomit. Overall, it was a somewhat uneventful deliverance, not like a Hollywood movie at all. Thank God! I helped him up. I looked at him, and said, "Will you play with fire again?"

"No," he said. "I'm sorry."

I knew he was apologizing to himself as well. His voice was stronger. He continued, "They were right: you did help me. Thank you."

"No problem. I'm just your friendly neighborhood vampire slayer," I said with a nervous laugh.

As he looked at me, I realized how beautiful and light his eyes were. They were a royal blue and almost iridescent. Amazing, I thought. I remembered that before the deliverance, they were dark brown, almost black. He turned around and walked into the night. I never saw him again. Now, all I was waiting for was for Linda Blair to approach me.

"What in the holy hell had just happened?" I said aloud. I walked over to the table where my friends' conversation had changed to the subject of human rights and animal rights. "Hello!" I shouted. "Did you see what just happened?"

"No," one friend exclaimed. "We were wondering where you went?"

"Went? I was just over there," and I pointed to the corner of the patio where other people were now seated. "Didn't you see the tall guy with bushy red hair?" Both friends looked at me with blank stares.

"Darrin," the other friend said, "you told us you were going to the bathroom. That was over a half hour ago. We were about to go find you."

"What?" I said—and then stopped. I realized what had happened. No one was meant to see what had just transpired. "Never mind," I said, with a sigh, and sat down. They quickly went on with their discussion. I sipped on my cold latte.

What a story, yes? I'm still flabbergasted every time I think back on it. My initiation into spiritual deliverance work proved to me that no matter how we let ourselves explore the dark side, there is always a pinpoint of light somewhere shining within us to guide us home. This story also points to the fact that we are affected by the energy and intention of the choices we make, good or bad. In the case of this young man, he had chosen to open the window to dark archetypes and chaos elementals. He became overcome by their influence due to his willing participation. His experience was a dramatic example of how thought-forms affect us, which helps us to understand how powerful we are. By choosing differently, this young man turned his life around to the acceptance of his true nature as a child of God. Remember that any religion, ritual, or practice that calls for you to dishonor your spiritual integrity causes the separation of you from your spiritual power.

My spiritual deliverance work has shown me the negative results from the use of black magic and practices of negatively centered rituals. They never reap the benefits of true power, which is divine power. You reap only what you sow, and negative energy attracts negative energy. Don't get me wrong, I enjoy watching the pop culture stories of vampires like those in "Twilight" and "True Blood," but we are talking about real acts of spiritual crises when it comes to encountering dark archetypes. When you have not firmed up your spiritual foundation, it's easy to search for power and acceptance from something outside of yourself. This young man finally discovered what he was truly made of, and I hope he continues to live with the divine privilege of authentic spiritual power.

## THE DARK FORCES AND THE SATAN ARCHETYPE

This is a good time to enter into a discussion of what the dark forces are and what we call "Satan" truly is. The Judeo-Christian belief describes Satan as a fallen angel, hell-bent on interfering and distorting God's divine plan. First, it is important to note that there is only one essential force in the universe and that is Divine Love, our Mother/Father God. The dark force, or the Satan archetype, is a force that is self-absorbed in its illusion that it is more powerful than God. The illusion of individual power creates separateness between God and Man. Throughout this chapter, we have been talking about that very thing. We misperceive our direction in life when we believe we are separated from the one true source of all life, Divine Love. The existence and reality of evil in our minds and in the world is fed by misperceptions of a lower state of awareness. Edgar Cayce explains the process of evil and its beginnings very clearly in his readings, on page 212 of *The Edgar Cayce Primer* by Herbert Puryear:

In the beginning, celestial beings. We have first the Son, then the other sons or celestial beings that are given their force and power. Hence that force which rebelled in the unseen forces (or in spirit) that came into activity, was that influence which has been called Satan, the Devil, the Serpent; they are One. That of *rebellion*!

Hence, when man in any activity rebels against the influences of good he harkens to the influence of evil rather than the influence of good . . .

Evil is rebellion, God is the Son of Life, of Light, of Truth; and the Son of Light, of Life, of Truth, came into physical being to demonstrate and show and lead the way for man's ascent to the power of good over evil in a material world.

As there is, then, a personal savior, there is the personal devil.                                                          262-52

These are very powerful words of explanation here. I believe that Cayce is referring to the Satan archetype (Fear) and then, of course, to the Son of God (Love). Jesus is the master of masters and is also the embodiment of spiritual deliverance or exorcism. Therefore, when you summon the divine archetype of Jesus Christ, you call for the power and the presence within you of Divine Love in all its glory. As Cayce explained, Jesus incarnated to show us that we are all are children of the most high. We have the resources within us to overcome evil and see the truth, that of being good and whole in every way.

Cayce confirms in his teachings, as does Master Ron Roth, that none of these evil forces has any power over us except what we allow by way of our own thoughts and intentions. We can make ourselves vulnerable by being out of sync or attunement with the Divine through thoughts, beliefs, and practices that engulf us in lower vibrational energies. In the Cayce readings, we are told that during the time of Genesis, the first creation of our spiritual selves, we were created in the image and likeness of God.

We were created as perfect spiritual beings in oneness with the Source, the Mother/Father God. We were blessed with the same creative powers as the source, fully embodying the right of co-creation along with God. Cayce goes on to explain that some souls, in the spirit of rebellion, wanted to be Gods, apart from God, who is the one and only Source. Through God's love we have been blessed by experiencing a spiritual evolution, and we are still progressing onward and upward internally to return to the source of all creation. I would suggest you read *Edgar Cayce's Origin and Destiny of Man* by Lytle W. Robinson, for more information on the story of creation and our soul's evolution.

## THE PITFALLS OF CONTACT AND COMMUNICATION WITH SPIRIT

There are many ways other than self-indulgence that allow someone to open the door to negative energy in fear. When making choices from a limited understanding of your spiritual resources, areas such as drug and alcohol addictions, black magic, Ouija boards, divination tools, and even mediumship might open doors to negative energies. Any practice of calling in spirits or energies might be taking a risk. I don't encourage people to open themselves up to spirits without proper training in how to navigate and discern the spirit realms. Beware those who say there are no such things as negative spirits. That kind of thought system might open a door for possession, and I have seen those cases take place again and again. I don't encourage the use of tarot cards or "spirit boards" because any tools that you might use as far as divination or "spirit contact" may be tampered with by outside energy sources. If you feel the need to use something like tarot cards, always ask the white light of the Holy Spirit to bless the cards. (Please refer to the white light technique used within the "Meditation for a Master of Light" at the end of the first chapter.) As far as Ouija boards are concerned, my recommendation is *no way*! Spirit boards of any kind are nothing but portals, wide open for anything to enter. About fifty percent of the possession cases I have been called in on have been caused by someone's use of a Ouija board. Again, these are my thoughts on a subject that I have been dealing with for over fifteen years. Edgar Cayce also warned against the use of Ouija boards, calling them dangerous toys. According to Hugh Lynn Cayce, Edgar Cayce's son, Ouija boards were dangerous doorways to the unconscious. Ouija was not created with the intention of the divine will of release and healing, so its very nature in energy terms is chaotic and non–discerning. I might give the impression that these "games" have a mind of their own, but in essence, spirit boards were created for a certain purpose. Sadly, that purpose is not always the will of the highest good.

In my research for this chapter, I found a remarkable account of a woman who wrote Hugh Lynn Cayce many years ago with her concerns about a "haunting" feeling she had begun to sense after using a Ouija board. His reply is thorough and very much confirms my findings regarding the warnings about the use of spirit boards, automatic writing, and most divination tools in general. He wrote to the woman that many people get very excited by opening their unconscious selves, or that of others, with Ouija boards or other automatisms. First, if users are emotional or suggestive—and they may be unconscious of this fact—they might split their unconscious mind by use of Ouija or automatic writing. These tools provide a direct way for suppressed areas of the unconscious to take control. Second, if users frequently daydream and fantasize, the use of Ouija boards and automatic tools will allow their unconscious to create many characters that were famous, important, or romantic in past lives that they think they lived. This occurrence has to do with the ego, which might allow the suppressed areas of the unconscious to take control. He went on to explain that people who are psychic and make use of Ouija boards or automatic writing can short–circuit their line of psychic power. Hugh Lynn Cayce's discussion on this topic can be found in the first chapter of Part 3 of the A.R.E. Press' reprinted version of his book, *Venture Inward*, published originally in 1964.

Again, in my own words here: people may short–circuit their psychic power by allowing themselves to become addicted to the spirit board, cards, or other psychic tools while forgetting that their line of psychic power is always within themselves and directed by God. Psychic power should never be based solely on "tools" outside of ourselves.

Over the many years that I have done my psychic work and consultations, I have seen very damaging effects happen to clients and colleagues who are completely addicted to their "lines of spirit communication" via the spirit boards, tarot, other divination tools, or even mediumship. One friend could not start her day until she "read" the cards. Others dreamed up various fantasies about true loves coming via the "spirit guide" they contacted with their Ouija board. This addiction goes for psychic readings, as well. As I discussed earlier, people who become dependent upon psychics are what I call "psychic hoppers." They jump from one psychic to another, and they hope to hear what they wish for. Even when they do hear what they want to hear, they often visit another psychic to confirm what the previous one said. Insanity! I make it a rule, unless someone is dealing with a spiritual crisis and needs ministerial help, that I will only "read" a person one time. My goal is and forever shall be to help people rely on their own psychic power and their own link to God. Many people who run around looking for God as well as answers on the outside of themselves will continue until they see and accept the knowledge that God is with them. They are co-creators with this divinity. Any spirit guide, angel, or teacher with integrity will always remind you of that truth.

Taken from the Edgar Cayce readings, this phrase puts my intention for this chapter into complete perspective: " . . . Be *willing* to be led; not by *spirits*, but by the *spirit* of God—Good—Right!" (257-78)

# 5 Divine Love Consciousness

Spiritual healing is the awakening of the Divine Love Consciousness within the mind, body, and soul. Divine Love is the pure, limitless consciousness of God. Divine Love is our truest form of being. All fear that manifests dis-ease and deprivation within the being of a soul can be balanced and transformed by the remembrance and sustained practice of living the path of Divine Love. As Masters of Light, we are agents for Divine Love.

## DIVINE LOVE: THE ULTIMATE REALITY OF ONENESS

Divine Love is the pure essence of the Creator. It is limitless in its potential for wholeness, well-being, and healing. Divine Love is the free-flowing force that the Holy Spirit instills within the hearts of creation. Divine Love is the remembrance of our spiritual nature. *We are Divine Love.*

Divine Love is the spiritual makeup that we are fully embodying, and with great achievements, in the New Golden Age. Divine Love is the foundation for the work of all Masters of Light. The ultimate goal of co-creating the New Age of Enlightenment is to live, heal, and sustain Divine Love Consciousness for our planet and humankind. Psychic readings, spiritual psychotherapy, and any healing work should always be directed to the areas of life where Divine Love may not yet be awake.

As we become more conscious of Divine Love in our lives, we will demonstrate more regularly the ultimate reality of oneness. We will manifest oneness with ourselves, each other, and the universe. We are literally all the family of one soul. The idea of unity helps us begin to understand the importance of spiritual humanitarianism. Since Divine Love is the highest level of love that we can connect to within ourselves, we can pull this essential resource directly from our intentions and manifest its presence on earth. My favorite quote, which is found in Chapter 16, Section IV, "The Illusion and the Reality of Love," in *A Course in Miracles* is, "Your task is not to seek for love but merely to seek and find all of the barriers within yourself which you have built against it." Many of you who are reading this book have already been working subtly on your ability to let Divine Love flow into your life. But, as the main theme of this book has taught, we must not heal our inner selves and be content; we seek to heal our inner selves so that we may be channels and embodiments of that healing for others. Divine Love is to be awakened within the heart of every soul. Those awakened souls take that energy of love out into the world and help others awaken, as well. This joining is the foundation for our oneness with all things. If we all become aware of our connection to God and our ability to receive God's Divine Love, we will no longer feel that we are separated from anyone or anything. Everything flows in oneness from the outpouring of Divine Love.

*Divine Love reminds us that we are not separate from God or each other. We are all one soul family.*

The New Earth is the new ideal of our planet that is being created through us, and the more we open to Divine Love, the more we are able to shift with ease into a New Golden Age. Below, I have added some helpful prayers to awaken Divine Love in your life—and in your very being. Allow yourself to open, and receive, for then you will be ready to be the giver, also.

## SIMPLE PRAYER FOR DIVINE LOVE

Divine Love, be in my thoughts.
Divine Love, be in my words.
Divine Love, be in my actions.
Divine Love, be in my choices.
Divine Love, be in my relationships.
Divine Love, be in my work.
Divine Love, be in my life—today and every day.

## MEDITATION FOR DIVINE LOVE AND ONENESS

Close your eyes and relax. Take a few deep breaths and let
everything go. Imagine a spinning wheel of emerald green
energy centered in the middle of your chest. Take a deep
breath and breathe in that green, emerald energy. Now exhale. Feel the oxygen filling your lungs as you breathe in
another powerful dose of that green, light energy.

Next, begin to imagine within the spinning wheel of emerald light, a golden light—piercing through—expanding
and mixing with the emerald. Breathe in that powerful combination of energy. This is the golden light of Divine Love,
making its way into your life, magnifying your own loving
energy. As you breathe deeply and easily, you see within the
center of your chest a yin-yang combination of emerald green
and golden light. It is a perfect balance. You are at one with
yourself, everything, and everyone around you.

This vortex of energy within you is your unlimited source
of Divine Love. You may use this energy in every life situation, choice, and action. This energy is there for you to create
a firm foundation for your life. This energy is also your renewed source of compassion and charity. The souls you encounter will feel this vibrant, loving energy as it makes its
way from your heart center to theirs. They will have the
chance to awaken their own Divine Love and oneness merely
by remaining in your presence.

Take a few more deep breaths, allowing Divine Love to

set up a permanent residence within you. Feeling relaxed
and easy, you return to your sacred space, ready to share in
the love that has blessed you.

The goal for every master of light is to be a channel of the most high,
literally bringing heaven to earth. From this powerful expression of our
hearts, one by one, Divine Love becomes the sacred sovereign who rules
our destiny's direction. We are truly blessed to be living in such times.
We can and will be the sacred catalyst for true change, the dynamic
change that Divine Love is awakening within every soul on this planet.

Now that you have an understanding of the living presence of Divine Love, let's discuss its role in the spiritual healing of ourselves and
our planet. First, know that spiritual healing is a balancing of the energies within the body, mind, emotions, and soul. A major lesson in sci-
ence class, as Albert Einstein declared, is that energy cannot be created
or destroyed; it can only be changed from one form to another. You
have already read an aspect of this process in the spiritual deliverance
chapter. Since we are energy bodies first, true healing is the transformation of energy from a lower vibration to a higher vibration brought on
by Divine Love. Divine Love is the highest vibration—of which we were
created—received directly from the Source. So, the arousal of Divine
Love Consciousness can rebalance the body and transform fear back
into the natural state of love. From this energetic, alchemical process,
the role of spiritual healing is simply to transform fear into love. Learning about this transformation is the basis for my spiritual healing re-
treats and services.

There are only two energies in the universe—those of love and fear.
We are complete reflections of the creative universe, so within us is the
potential for two kinds of energy consciousness to reside: love and fear.
Fear is not God-created. Fear is a perverted energy created by our fall
from God's co-creative nature—a fall from Divine Love Consciousness
to egocentric consciousness. Once we found ourselves lost in the shuffle
over the ages, fear was more and more directed from our sense of loss,
selfish power, and grief. Fear then turned itself into many faces such as
anger, hate, and greed. We found ourselves in a difficult situation with
no easy escape, for sure. When the human body is bombarded by fear

and its many traits for a long period of time, it begins to weaken the physical, mental, and emotional body. Before you know it, you have become unbalanced with dis-ease that presents itself in many forms. For this situation, I would highly recommend reading Edgar Cayce's works on health and healing available from the A.R.E. Press as well as a wonderful a little book called *Heal Your Body* by Louise L. Hay. Both of these teachers provide great insights concerning the transformation of thoughts and their effects on our health.

## RAISING YOUR VIBRATION TO DIVINE LOVE CONSCIOUSNESS

Divine Love is the catalyst for healing and enlightenment. The majority of people who travel from around the world to attend my healing services or to obtain private healing sessions want the same thing—to be healed and to know their life purpose. When you raise your vibration through an active shift in your thoughts from fear to love, healing and enlightenment are the natural by-products of the shift. This transformation is the role of spiritual healing. A healer is simply a doorway between the energy of Divine Love and that of the person who requires healing.

When I hear from students or clients, "I need a healing!", what I'm really being told is, "I want to raise my vibration. I no longer want to experience fear as my prominent emotion."

The relationship between the client and healer is a two-way street that must be a temporary partnership of divine union. The healing energy that takes place through a true healer happens because he or she is conscious in his or her vibrational frequency; during the healing session, the healer is in harmony with Divine Love. That transference of energy helps to raise the vibration of the client to the true higher source. Like attracts like. In essence, the healer is merely helping to awaken the healing potential within another person. It is nothing special; it's based on the intention of both parties. One gives and the other receives.

I have been asked many times, does a person have to believe in the healer to be healed? Not really. Many people who have attended my healing services have walked in with a closed mind to the process. My belief is that they approached for a reason, and their higher self turned out to be stronger than their skepticism. I'm not here to prove any-thing—merely to be God's channel. Being a channel for Divine Love should be the intention for any spiritual healer.

If you want to prove something or shout, "Look how powerful I am," you are not representing God's healing presence—only your own spot-light. These "charmer" types of people tend to burn out fast. In my nu-merous years of doing this work, I have learned to stay clear of people who label their healing work. They coin special, long-winded names and copyright them to the world; this is pure, egocentric nonsense. You can't label and box God's healing power. It is universal in its nature and is available to everyone. No one person has a special technique that is better than any other. Let the love flow, and stop trying to make it a "special only," as though it is buffet time at a Chinese restaurant.

Many years ago, I met a very well-known healer. His trade was that of a chiropractor, and through "wondrous" means, he received a "spe-cial" healing technique from extraterrestrial beings that only *he* could give and teach to others. Can you see where I'm heading with this story? We had mutual acquaintances, and he had wanted to meet me for some time. After his lecture, he walked up to me and shook my hand. He then reached into his side coat pocket and pulled out a flask. He gulped down a swallow. Scotch was his chosen spirit that day. He put the flask back in his pocket and said, "How did you like *me?*"

I could feel my Sagittarian fire rising within me. I was not only ap-palled by his inflated ego but also outraged at the total disrespect to the real work of healing. Remaining very calm and tactful, I replied, "I've seen better shows at sea world."

As I walked off, I heard him cry out, "You want to have dinner?"

I kept walking.

There are just as many deceitful artists out there selling their snake oils as there are authentic healers and psychics who are imparting as much of Divine Love's essence as they can. Discernment is important, here. It is time for us to ask the Holy Spirit to strengthen our gift of discernment, as you read earlier, and shine the light on what is good and true for us regarding our healing. It's very easy to fall into the traps of good marketing campaigns when it comes to healing. Now, don't misunderstand me. I am in favor of trying different processes to learn about your healing potential. I draw the line, however, when it comes to promoting the energy of healing as something "special." I have seen many people with a need to be "special" flock to celebrity psychics and healers to learn "their" way.

They also want to be popular by association. "If I take this famous person's class and am listed on their Web site as a certified practitioner, then I'm special, too. I'll get noticed!"

I have learned from many excellent teachers in my life and have received certificates that went right into the trash can on the way out the door. I don't need a piece of paper to tell me that I'm a healing agent for God. I use what feels right to me and leave the rest behind. I'm always organic in my spiritual work. I'm not a sheep and never have been that kind of follower. Learn all you can about opening up to God's presence, but don't become attached to fancy healing labels and techniques. Be the spiritual being God intended you to be. Don't be an impostor who copies someone else. If you want "certification," that is fine, but please know that a certain technique is not your source for healing. Let the Divine Love flow. You have a special relationship with Divine Love Consciousness that money can't buy. It's free and free-flowing to you.

# 6 Earth Healing Consciousness

Well-being and total wellness is our body's natural state. The Creator formed our physical vehicles to perform and stabilize with ease on this planet. It is our body's natural response to heal and balance itself. In most cases, when we allow our negative attitudes, unhealthy emotions, or even pharmaceutical toxins to get in the way of our body's natural state of well-being, we undermine our health. I'd like to discuss what I call "Earth Healing Consciousness." When it comes to true healing with Divine Love, there is an essential requirement of maintaining a balance between heaven and earth. Divine Love Consciousness and Earth Healing Consciousness work hand in hand as a marriage of the physical and the spiritual. We must have our bodies' energetic roots (the lower three chakras) submerged deeply in the earth as the upper energies (the upper three chakras) stretch up to the heavens for our spiritual nourishment. Our heart center, which cycles everything in harmony, is our bridge of balance. As above, so below; as within, so without.

Earth was created to nurture us and provide us with everything we need as far as food, water, medicinal earth-based remedies, and basic living essentials. A major cause in our health challenges—physical, mental, and emotional—is based in our lack of earth consciousness. We were meant to live in union with this planet, not to divide and conquer it. We must return to living in harmony with its natural flow. We are unhealthy because we have separated ourselves from earth's energetic nutrients. Many are doing their part to raise earth consciousness awareness with the green movement, environmental and animal rights, and the organic food trades. But this work is not enough. As Masters of Light, we have to bring that earth consciousness back into our personal energy systems by connecting and grounding to it. Earth Healing Consciousness must be a lifestyle. This is part of our mission as initiators of the New Earth. Grounding is an absolute essential to embody Divine Love in our healthy bodies. We need to have strong physical, mental, and emotional stamina that is firmly planted into the energies of the earth in order to fully channel our light.

I see many people in my business who hover in the clouds. Without grounding, they fizzle out and transmit a "flighty" sense to their personality. They are like a leaf that floats wherever the wind blows. They contribute little energy to their destiny and the creation of it. We must master a firmly balanced foundation and allow our body to be in constant flow with positive energy. Many of us have felt the presence of being around someone who is truly balanced. There is a sense of peace around that person. An inner calm vibrates from their souls, and we wonder how do they do it? Simply put, it involves an ongoing practice of being grounded in the earth's energies while lifting our metaphoric branches to the heavens.

As with anything, there may be a pendulum's swing to this idea. Just as some might appear to be too far "up in the clouds," others may seem too staunch in their groundedness. They are not flexible; instead, they have dug a hole and filled it with cement. They don't budge from their perceptions.

Below is a listing of desirable grounding traits that many of us have experienced throughout the different stages of our lives. The goal is to sustain a balanced, grounded nature as much as possible on a daily basis. Again, to reach for or to embody Divine Love fully, we must have a good grounding. This is information that I have gathered over the years from my private healing practice. I have observed these traits again and again. If you make an authentic spiritual practice a priority in your life, creating a balanced, grounded nature is quite achievable.

**Grounded Traits**
- Calm personality
- Non-reaction to life events
- Good common sense
- Strong physical stamina
- Overall good health
- Open mind and open heart
- Humanitarian actions
- Reliability
- Food consciousness
- Team player
- Nature and outdoor enthusiast
- Compromiser
- Animal Lover
- Financial stability

**Overly-Grounded Traits**
- Unwavering attitude
- Persona who is always right
- Inability to accept others' truth
- Inability to compromise
- Lack of empathy
- Complaining nature
- Cynical and critical
- Workaholic
- Miserly
- Obsessive need for detail
- Control freak

**Ungrounded Traits**
- Flighty

- Unable to make decisions
- Prone to injuries and accidents
- Lacks intuitive sense
- Unreliable
- Fast-food junkie
- Prone to laziness
- Lacks life direction
- Financially and emotionally unstable
- Has a "who cares" attitude
- Prone to constant colds and allergies
- Gives no attention to details

All of us at some point in time may recognize these traits within ourselves. Some folks remain fairly constant in one nature for their entire life. As we live within the New Golden Age, it is more and more apparent that we stay balanced in our grounding in order to be conscious co-creators with the Divine. If we are overly grounded or not grounded enough, we cannot be clear channels of light. Also, nothing will manifest fully in our life, so making a dream or an intention come true becomes almost impossible.

When you plant a seed, you need the earth, the sun, and water to help it grow. It's the same with our ability to co-create with the Divine. We need to ground into the living nutrients of the earth in order for the spiritual power activated within us to manifest into our reality. As the bloom of a flower opens to the sun, so does our destiny to the horizon of our life path. Divine Love Consciousness is essential in understanding our grounding and its properties for the work of spiritual healing. When healing takes place within one's being, it begins to balance the body's energies—rooting us to the earth—and helps us reach our creative energies upward into harmony. Healing on all levels is harmony, balance, grounding, and perfect well-being. This balance is our natural state.

I have witnessed the Holy Spirit's work as it awakens Divine Love within attendees at my assemblies. As people come to receive healings, I can feel spiritual energy move from the top of their heads, shooting straight down into the earth and then rising back up again. It cycles over and over until balance is achieved. Many people have found that their changes—whether physical, emotional, or mental—are greatly relieved by this process of Divine Love's integration with the earth consciousness. It's a wonderful sight to witness and a very memorable experience. A woman who attended one of my healing services approached the podium for me to lay hands on her. I am a channel for healing, so my process of work in this situation is very simple. I lay my right hand on the top of the head, and reach out my left hand, palm up. "Come, Holy Spirit" are my only words. When I apply this practice, I become a human x-ray, and it feels as though I am able to see the health challenges through the Holy Spirit's point of view. As the spirit moved throughout the body of this woman, I felt heaviness below her waist. Then, the spirit moved rapidly through the top of her head and back to her hips. She collapsed. She seemed to be in a very peaceful state. This experience happens at times when the Holy Spirit is doing some major rebalancing. She will put the body in a Zen-like state to perform psychic and energetic healing. I tell my staff to leave people alone when they fall out. Let the spirit do her work; don't interfere. When the woman arose a few moments later, she looked completely refreshed. A friend of hers walked over to help her up, due to her severe hip pain. The woman looked surprised as she stood up without any help. She walked around and then approached me. She hugged me and stated she had not been able to walk without a cane for years. I had not noticed the cane when she walked up to receive the healing. When I'm in my healing state of awareness, I never see health problems—only a person's potential to heal. The woman was very earthy in her nature but was very staunch in her attitude. She was also a control freak who hated any kind of change with a passion. Years of living this lifestyle had literally weighed her down and crushed her hips. She was so stuck in her beliefs that she was compressing her lower skeletal system. When the spirit moved through her, it shifted the energy and broke the chains she had created for herself. Divine Love flowed. She was walking without pain, and she was ready to heal. Her case is a great example of being overly grounded.

Let me remind you that this healing was not something that happened to her from an outside source; it was something that she opened up within herself. She was working with her own intention to heal.

With the Holy Spirit, Divine Love flowed through her and balanced her energies between heaven and earth. Once the healing and balancing has taken place, it is up to the individual to maintain it. If you choose to fall back into the same thought system that added to creating the imbalances in the first place, your body will reflect that attitude and return to an unhealthy state. So, maintain your spiritual workout every day.

There are many ways to make sure you stay grounded in your everyday life. First, set your intention every morning to visualize your body's energy rooting itself into the green and luscious earth with your arms as branches reaching to the sky, enveloped by sunshine and fresh air. I have provided a simple prayer for grounding in this section. If visualization is a challenge for you, take as many nature walks as you can during your week. Go somewhere with a variety of trees. Trees are not only a great example of perfect grounding, but they can also assist you in grounding your own energy. The next time you are outdoors, locate a tree that you feel drawn to. I love oak trees, personally. Also, make sure you find one that will not lather you with sap kisses! I have provided a great exercise you can do on your nature walks, and it is called Tree Deeksha.

## TREE DEEKSHA

The word "Deeksha" means "gift" or "transfer." It's derived from ancient Sanskrit and is considered to be the purest form of a blessing from God and your higher self. In relation to trees, you can receive "Deeksha" freely from a willing tree. When you are in major need of grounding and are in too much of a difficult mental or emotional state to ground yourself, do this exercise. It will help to balance and energize you. It is a quick jump-start like having an energy drink.

When you find a tree that you feel drawn to, make sure to ask its permission, silently, to receive Deeksha from it. Trees are our ancient companions and must be held in great respect. When a tree gives me its consent, I feel a light, lifting sensation in my solar plexus, and I know it is acceptable to continue. When you feel that a tree is letting you into its space, turn your back to it and lean your entire body on the trunk. You may sit on the ground with your back to the base of the tree, as well.

You need do nothing but close your eyes and breathe deeply and easily. You will soon feel the grounding energy of the tree raise your energy up to match its own perfectly balanced energy. Spiritually and energetically, you become one with the tree. Pure, Earth Healing Consciousness is awakened. Take as long as you need. When you feel the stress and flighty energy leave your body and you are more relaxed, the blessing has been given. I love tree Deeksha! Make sure to give your thanks to the tree before you leave. Repeating this exercise outdoors will assist your ability to mentally visualize the tree grounding exercise when you must stay indoors.

Many years ago I had my astrology chart prepared and found out that I had absolutely no earth elements in my chart. There were no earth signs in any houses. The elements and planets of fire and water were the only energies vibrating in my system. That explained a lot: "I have steam heat!" I must have sensed my own process for making up for the lack of earth in my chart over the years. I'm drawn to earth-colored clothing. I always wear black or brown shoes. I have close friends with earthy personalities—I'm drawn to them.

If you find that your traits are frequently ungrounded at times, just shift the colors you wear to those of earth tones. Color affects your energy and helps in the process of grounding. From personal experience, it works.

## PRAYER FOR PERFECT ENERGETIC BALANCE

To end this section, I have included a simple grounding prayer. As I always say, when all else fails, pray.

Come, Holy Spirit. Guide me into complete and perfect balance with Earth Healing Consciousness. I ask that you please balance and restore all of my energy centers to their original vibration in league with Divine Love. I open to receive healing on all levels of my being. I feel my body's sacred energy root deeply into the earth and stretch high into the heavens. I am in perfect balance. I am perfectly grounded. Holy Spirit, thank you.

# 7 Spiritual Healing

I'm often asked, "Can I be a spiritual healer?" My answer is that everyone is a healer in some form or fashion. You are a healer when you smile at a stranger. You are a healer when you hold someone's hand while he is in pain. You are a healer when you say a kind word. You are a healer because you wake up every day to greet the universe in all of its glory. You are a healer when your intentions are to shine your inner light to the world. It is apparent that as a Master of Light who is co-creating our part of enlightenment on this planet, spiritual healing is an essential component to our mission. Let me emphasize here that spiritual healing does not refer to possessing magic hands that heal the masses of their inflictions. You may have wanted to lay hands on a person and witness her fall to the floor in rapture while wheelchairs and crutches fall to the ground as you pass by. Unbelievably, there are still people who expect to see spiritual healing happen in this dramatic fashion. Healing may be subtle or dramatic depending on the guidance and intention of the Holy Spirit.

I'm taking you into the subtle approach. I'm also frequently asked if there is a difference between a healer and a spiritual healer. The answer is no. All healing is spiritually based. Even a doctor who performs brain surgery has angels that help to guide the process. Everything consists of energy, and there is nothing on the planet that is not surrounded by some sort of spiritual energy.

I'm often asked by people if I would teach them to be a healer or to be psychic. I don't believe that a person can be taught to be a healer, or even less, a psychic. These gifts represent a higher calling, ordained by God. One can be taught authentic practices and exercises to open up to healing and psychic potential for everyday life. If you find that destiny takes you further into psychic healing as a practice, your heart will accommodate the right time and place for that work to become a reality for you. I was taught by the best healers and teachers over the years, and their wisdom provided wonderful stepping-stones. My best lessons, however, came from hands-on experience plus trial and error. That's why I'm not going to teach you anything about healing except for the process of opening and invoking the power of Divine Love to awaken within you. The Holy Spirit is the teacher and educator. She will guide you fully into healing as a practice if that's your contract with God. The goal is never to *become* a healer or a psychic. The goal is to heal and be healed, and to allow yourself to be used as an embodiment and an agent of Divine Love. Let whatever life has you doing at this moment be expanded by mastering the light—and let the light live through you by example and practice.

I once heard a colleague tell a story about a friend of hers who was a natural masseuse. He had no training but was very intuitive in his ability to massage the body while locating all of the trouble spots and smoothing them out, perfectly. One day, he proclaimed to my colleague that he was going to massage school to become certified.

Her first reaction was to say, "No! You will lose your natural ability."

He felt he was not good enough and wanted the "right" techniques from a certified school. After his course of studies, his massages were never the same. He chose to practice by someone else's standards, giving up his natural instinct. The moral of the story is to take the opportunity to educate yourself as much as you can, but don't lose your natural instinct and intuitive voice when it comes to any type of healing practice. Trust your inner voice, and don't suppress it to any system of thought or teacher that claims to know more than you do. Take information that feels right, and leave the rest behind. You are born with amazing gifts that are all your own.

You are all natural healers. You can't become what you already are. Just allow yourself to accept it. What the ego tricks us into thinking is that we want to be an all-powerful, certified healer. Stop and reconsider. Be the embodiment you were born to be and not what the glamour factory of the new age, pop-culture machine dangles in front of your face. Being the stubborn Sagittarian I am, I rejected many nonsensical marketing and media campaigns for my book. I would not be stamped as America's new psychic star. I would not "show off" my powers by giving mini-readings during interviews. I was turned down for many events and expos because I would not do gallery readings or "perform" for the masses. I wanted to teach and to heal. Some in the business told me that my desire was not popular or marketable enough. Something seemed very wrong. Nevertheless, I am happy to march to the beat of my own healing drum. I want you to do the same. Don't follow the herd. Lead your own life, and let God be the only energy that directs you. Regard spiritual healing as a natural attribute of your life. Take out the "oooh and ahhh," and let healing be something as natural as wearing clothing for you.

The purpose of a healer is to be a font of Divine Love Consciousness. In essence, this entire book is a spiritual healing primer. We can take the cues from our higher self concerning what we learn from others and what we learn from ourselves. As we continue to master the light within us and focus on the goal of enlightenment for the planet, healing becomes an everyday practice. Every day we have the opportunity to give Deeksha or blessings to everything and everyone we encounter. We learn to bless others just by thinking of them surrounded by Divine Love. Even when certain folks offend us at times, think to yourself, "You are Divine Love." Each thought of Divine Love sent to another person is a network of energy that builds over time, creating a web of light everywhere we go. Eventually, the people we have blessed begin to open and awaken, too. At that time, they will begin the process of blessing and creating their webs of light. Masters of Light are reborn every day just by sending thoughts of Divine Love to one another.

# 8 The Healing Formulas

*I* have added what I call healing formulas for you to use as aids in your healing process or practice. Please know that these formulas are *not* intended to replace your doctor's or therapist's guidance or diagnosis. Please use them as additions to your regimens for health and well-being. These formulas are simply aids to help you to open and receive Divine Love Consciousness. Anyone can use these formulas for themselves or for someone else. Remember that a healer's code of ethics is to always ask permission from the person who is receiving healing before pronouncing a formula.

Pure intention and direction, in union with Divine Love, is our right to decree—through the power of the Holy Spirit—the living breath of God within us. When you are saying these formulas, please note that you are not casting a spell or doing magic. You are simply directing your mind and heart to be open channels for spiritual healing. You are, with right intention, opening yourself up to allow Divine Love to flow through you to any area or person who needs a tune-up or a reminder of his or her own healing potential. These formulas are nothing special, nor are they a great secret used only by masters. Remember to stay grounded, and do not allow the ego to make you believe that you are the messiah. Simply allow yourself to be an open channel. Remember, we are all healers to some degree.

As previously stated, these formulas are aids and not a new technique. This format has worked for me for many years of my practice, and I want to share it with you. Please feel free to accommodate and shift the wording to fit your own healing process and spiritual path. Just remember, keep it simple, and focus on Divine Love as your source. Do not attach yourself to the outcome when using these formulas. When the Holy Spirit directs Divine Love Consciousness, she knows where and how the process of healing needs to be directed. Remember that you are only the channel. Let the spirit direct. Stay focused only on being a clear channel for the Holy Spirit to move through you. Like water being poured through a clear glass spout, let it flow. Don't allow yourself to be attached to the need for proof that someone was healed. Pronounce the formula, and know that spirit is doing her work. Sometimes healing is subtle, and sometimes it's dramatic. Either way, attach not. Just be.

I always recite the formulas out loud and three times each. Reciting a sacred phrase or word three times helps the mind and heart to open. It will raise your consciousness to meet the higher vibration contained in the formula. Like chanting the different names of God repeatedly to enhance enlightenment, this format follows the same line of thought. Also, the power of three has always been sacred: Father, Son, and Holy Spirit; Maid, Mother, and Crone; or Mind, Body, and Spirit have been triads of power for centuries. Also, if for some reason you can't speak these aloud, saying them to yourself will work, as well. It's not as important how you perform them as it is to have your good intention behind them.

There is no need to touch the person being healed. If it's a formula for you or for someone else, simply rest your left hand on your heart and hold your right hand up to the heavens. This gesture is symbolic of spiritual power being given to the right hand from our heart center, which is the doorway for the Holy Spirit and Divine Love Consciousness. The right hand, raised up palm outward, represents the power that is received.

As I have previously mentioned, spiritual power wells up from within you and does not originate from anything outside of you. The formulas are written so that you are guiding along with the Holy Spirit as you recite them. You're not asking for a healing; you are directing it, girded by your full spiritual self-esteem. When people ask for a healing, it is often requested with desperation and pleading. Dis-ease can make us feel hopeless, but it's the spirit within that is the healer. We have to be strong enough with our words and thoughts to release its presence within our being.

**Note:** *Make sure before reciting any of the formulas to use the Spiritual Cleansing and Protection Prayer from the following chapter called "The Invocations." This cleansing will help clear out your auric energy field from any negative debris or outside influence, paving the way for right intention and spiritual protection for healing.*

### Healing Formula for the Physical Body
*(Examples: cancer, AIDS, diabetes, heart disease, muscular pain, headaches, etc.)*
Energy and consciousness of (insert physical ailment), through the power and presence of the Holy Spirit, I release you and unbind you. I turn you from negative to positive, and I transform you back to Divine Love Consciousness. *Repeat three times.*

### Healing Formula for the Mental Body
*(Examples: PTSD, OCD, sleep disorders, bipolar disorder, worry, mental anxiety etc.)*
Energy and consciousness of (insert mental ailment), through the power and presence of the Holy Spirit, I release you and unbind you. I turn you from negative to positive, and I transform you back to Divine Love Consciousness. *Repeat three times.*

### Healing Formula for the Emotional Body
*(Examples: depression, hopelessness, heartbreak, emotional anxiety, anger, grief, etc.)*
Energy and consciousness of (insert emotional ailment),

through the power and presence of the Holy Spirit, I release you and unbind you. I turn you from negative to positive, and I transform you back to Divine Love Consciousness. *Repeat three times.*

### Healing Formula for the Spiritual Body
*(Examples: inflexible trauma, fear of the unknown, spiritual abandonment, lack, worthlessness, victimization, etc.)*
Energy and consciousness of (insert spiritual ailment), through the power and presence of the Holy Spirit, I release you and unbind you. I turn you from negative to positive, and I transform you back to Divine Love Consciousness. *Repeat three times.*

Below, I have added more healing formulas that are centered specifically on energy unbalances that I have found to be particular challenges to our spiritual growth. I have observed these challenges in over seventeen years of giving readings. These formulas should be recited by the individual, if at all possible, due to their specific focus. If for some reason you are reciting it for someone else, feel free to insert the name of the individual you are directing the formula to, and recite it in the third person.

### Healing Formula for Lack and Scarcity
Energy and consciousness of lack and scarcity, through the power and presence of the Holy Spirit, I release you and unbind you. I turn you from negative to positive, and I transform you back to Divine Love Consciousness.

All my needs are met. The universe supports me in every area of my life. I am open to receive and open to accept the support from the universe. Through Divine Love, I know this to be true. And so it is. *Repeat three times.*

### Healing Formula for Safety and Security
Energy and consciousness of safety and security, through the power and presence of the Holy Spirit, I release you and un-

bind you. I turn you from negative to positive, and I transform you back to Divine Love Consciousness.

I am safe and secure in my world. My life is mine to create. I'm a child of the most high, and I am wrapped in a blanket of comfort. God loves me. I am loved, pure and simple. Through Divine Love, I know this to be true. And so it is. *Repeat three times.*

### Healing Formula for Loss and Grief
Energy and consciousness of loss and grief, through the power and presence of the Holy Spirit, I release you and unbind you. I turn you from negative to positive, and I transform you back to Divine Love Consciousness.

I surrender my life to Divine Will. I let go of persons, places, or things that no longer serve my highest good. I let go of the pain of separation, and I know that my soul fills those places within me that are empty. I am healed by Divine Love. This surrender and letting go in my life opens the door for better and brighter circumstances. I love my "self," and I know that I can take care of myself. God loves me. I am loved, pure and simple. Through Divine Love, I know this to be true. And so it is. *Repeat three times.*

### Healing Formula for Addiction
Energy and consciousness of (insert addictions), through the power and presence of the Holy Spirit, I release you and unbind you. I turn you from negative to positive, and I transform you back to Divine Love Consciousness.

I no longer need or desire your presence in my life. You are transformed and released, no longer controlling my mind and emotions. My body returns back into balance, and it is no longer energetically or chemically addicted to (insert addiction). And so it is. *Repeat three times.*

### Healing Formula for Co-Dependency
Energy and consciousness of co-dependency, through the

power and presence of the Holy Spirit, I release you and un-bind you. I turn you from negative to positive, and I transform you back to Divine Love Consciousness.

I no longer need or desire (insert name) to feel safe or better about myself. I listen to my own self-worth and intuition in my life. I love myself and know that I am emotionally secure, on my own. I reinstate the truth that a healthy relationship contains two whole people, secure and strong, vibrating on the same level. Co-dependent nature, you are transformed and released, no longer controlling my mind and emotions. My mind and emotions return back into balance and are no longer energetically or emotionally co-dependent to (insert name). My relationships to others and myself are in perfect balance. And so it is. *Repeat three times.*

# The
# Invocations

The act of invoking the spiritual power within you is one of the most intimate connections you could ever have with Pure Divine Love. Every time we pray and ask for the power of God to enter our lives, we step closer and closer to the truth that we are one with the creative source of all things.

These invocations may be used whenever you feel the need. Invocations are another tool for your use as a Master of Light. The healing formulas are more specific to personal healing challenges, and the invocations are more universal in nature. Their purpose is to open you up to spiritual power. Verbalizing aloud or reading silently, these commanding words will help strengthen your direct link to the divine spiritual resources within and all around you.

Each Invocation is associated with a specific topic or challenge mentioned in this book. I'll also include invocations to help reinstate spiritual power in many life areas such as relationships, career, health, and finances. As we co-create our lives in this New Golden Age, we must use the power we have been blessed with to raise our vibrations and catapult this planet even further into spheres of divine love.

## INVOCATION FOR SPIRITUAL
## CLEANSING AND PROTECTION

This invocation will help you open to the spiritual protection within you. By calling for these divine archetypal energies, you will feel safe and secure in your world, and you will know that the Divine will always watch around and behind you to protect what you can't see.

> I ask the *Band of Mercy* to please remove all lost souls and unclean spirits that may be attached to, affecting, or influencing me (for another person, insert the name), my family, my house and property, and all that I have ownership of. I ask this through the power and presence of the *Christ light* within me, and I thank thee.
>
> I ask the appropriate angelic protectors to please remove all negative entities and energies that may be attached to, affecting, or influencing me, my family, my house and property, and all that I have ownership of. I ask this through the power and presence of the *Christ light* within me, and I thank thee.
>
> I ask the *Archangel Michael* and his legions to please remove all negative entities, energies, thought-forms, and influences that may be attached to or affecting me, my family, my house and property, and all that I have ownership of. I ask this through the power and presence of the *Christ light* within me, and I thank thee.
>
> I now ask the *Holy Spirit* to please guide and protect me. Please dissolve and disperse any and all remaining fearful, negative, or residual energies; and replace them with your unlimited light, love, and grace. I also request this protection for my family, my house and property, and all that I have ownership of. I ask this through the power and presence of the *Christ light* within me, and I thank thee.

# DEFINITIONS OF TERMS FOR THIS INVOCATION

**Band of Mercy:** a group of enlightened souls assigned to those who have died to assist them as they cross to the other side. Being ministers and healers, they specialize in the careful transition through the light of souls that are lost or earthbound. The essence of their work is making the transition of souls between worlds as easy as possible.

**The Archangel Michael:** the sword and shield of God. The Archangel Michael and his legions help in the removal of negative energies and entities. Michael is also called on for protection and strength during times of immense fear, chaos, and confusion.

**Christ Light/Consciousness:** Jesus the Christ was the master of masters. Jesus walked the earth as an embodiment of the union with the Divine. He guides us to open our hearts to the Christ Consciousness/Divine Union which is a force of God's unconditional love and wisdom. The Master Jesus reminds us that we are children of the most high, and the kingdom of heaven is within us.

**The Holy Spirit:** the living breath of the Mother/Father God. She is the anointer of wisdom, grace, spiritual awakening, and Pure Divine Love. The word holy means "whole," and spirit is equivalent to "being." So, the Holy Spirit can be thought of as a force pushing all existence toward wholeness. When this energy is called, it helps sustain balance and restore peace, bringing wholeness back to the individual or a situation. The Holy Spirit blesses the sacred contract with Divine Love and envelops us in the protective power of this prayer.

## INVOCATION FOR GOLDEN AGE AWARENESS

This invocation's objective is to guide you into the awareness of your importance and mission in the New Golden Age of Enlightenment. You are a minister of light. When you re-remember who you are, you will realize that you have a purpose on this planet.

> Divine Holy Spirit, help me to remember my place in this universe as your channel and messenger. We are now living and breathing in the New Golden Age of Enlightenment. By

your ordination, I realize that I am a minister of light. I will live my life by the truth of my divinity and will be a beacon for those who sleep in the illusion of fear.

Holy Spirit, I know there are days when I, too, fall asleep and forget to see your sunrise within my heart. May those days be infrequent by the invocation of your power in my life today and every day. I am important and I am loved. With this reinstatement of my spiritual self-esteem, I know that my purpose is one of charity and love. No matter what I do or where I go, you are always guiding my hand to touch others with the gift of awakening and enlightenment. Holy Spirit, I thank you. Amen.

## INVOCATION OF THE HOLY SPIRIT

As you have seen throughout this book, the power and conscious-ness of the Holy Spirit is woven in and out of the teachings. The Holy Spirit, or the divine feminine, is truly the comforter and healer of all wounds. As previously stated, she pushes everything back into whole-ness and balance in our lives. This invocation encourages you to receive her presence in your daily life and spiritual practice.

Holy Spirit, fill my body, mind, and heart with your ever-lasting love. Your healing energy washes over me, bathing everything in light. I awaken to your voice as it guides my intuition today and every day. Make me a channel of your peace and wisdom, always reassuring me of my essential place in the universe as a minister of light. To you, I surren-der all areas of my life in which I continue to allow fear to reside. Through your grace, those areas are now balanced and purified, never to hide God's light from me again. I accept your blessing and healing, and I fully embody the awaken-ing that it offers me.

To you, I surrender any and all challenges in my health, relationships, and career. I know that you are the corrector of all misperceptions and that you will help me change my thinking from fear to love. From my correct thought, steeped in Divine Love, all ills are healed, all imbalance is balanced, and all dis-ease is eased.

Come, Holy Spirit, come. Amen.

## INVOCATION OF THE CHRIST CONSCIOUSNESS

The Christ Consciousness is that of complete union with the Divine. This invocation helps you restore and replenish your relationship with God and his or her child. We are all children of the most high. This invocation will metabolize that truth in your consciousness.

I invoke the Christ Consciousness within me. I open to the ultimate truth that I am a child of God and I am one with Divinity. I open my heart and mind to the essential teachings of Christ, which are those of love, forgiveness, and non-judgment. Through the ministering of the Holy Spirit, I will see my life as Christ did, as one of ultimate service and guidance to others. May I help every soul I meet know that he or she is divine and that nothing separates anyone from God's love. All of God's children are loved beyond measure. No matter the race, gender, or sexual orientation, we are made in God's image—perfect and whole. I accept this truth in my life through the inspiration of the Christ within me.

Dear God, thank you for the healing salvation of the Christ Consciousness, blessed by the Holy Spirit. In this prayer, I am in remembrance of my divinity today and every day. Amen.

## INVOCATION FOR HEALTH AND WELL-BEING

We all have the desire to be healthy. The well–being of our minds, bodies, and emotions is essential in the New Golden Age. There is such immense healing power within us that we must learn to call for this healing potential on a daily basis. Many of us continue to believe that healing is an outside job, when in fact it's the opposite. Healing begins with you. No matter what the challenge, simply invoking the Holy Spirit for healing begins the process of recovery on all levels.

> Come, Holy Spirit. Your healing balm bathes my physical body, my mental body, and my emotional body with everlasting purity. Any and all dis-ease is now balanced by your touch. Healing begins with the awareness of wholeness. And you, Holy Spirit, guide everyone back into a perfect wholeness and oneness with the Divine. My fears, my worries, and my hopelessness disappear with the awareness that you are my holy physician. You do not cover the pain or the dysfunction; you heal it and restore everything to God's perfect blueprint of health for me. You lead me with a guiding hand to the consciousness that brought me to this dis-ease. I see the illness, and I let it go. I let go of all emotional, mental, or physical ills that restrain me from your healing presence. I accept this healing today and every day. I let your holy breath of life fill me to the brim, overflowing and everlasting. Amen.

## INVOCATION FOR HEALTHY RELATIONSHIPS

We all have a desire for healthy relationships in our life. During this time of the great quickening, it is imperative for us to have relationships that are built on strong spiritual foundations. Whether your relationship is with a partner, lover, friend, or family member, each connection you have to another soul is there for a purpose. *A Course in Miracles* calls this soul–to–soul connection a "Holy Relationship." This invocation will encourage you to open your heart to relationships based on a higher consciousness and a deep commitment to a spiritual path, made even more powerful when united through Divine Love.

> Divine Holy Spirit, I open my heart to all the love that you have in store for me. I ask that you bless each and every relationship in my life as a holy encounter. Any former internal struggle with receiving love in my life is washed away by

your healing presence. I know that I do not have to seek for love in my life, for it is here with me right now. The light shining forth from my soul will attract only loving individuals who are vibrating to the same mystical power that you have bestowed upon me today. I let go of any hurt, anger, and resentment from past relationships. I know that those were powerful stepping stones to the realization of my own power. Holy Spirit, I know that I deserve all the love you have to offer me. I accept this truth today and every day. I am love, and I am loved. Amen

## INVOCATION FOR FINANCIAL BLESSINGS

Financial stress is an epidemic. I have always said that if something is a major stressor in your life, then it is also the most powerful. The truth is that money is not the culprit here. The perceptions and intentions behind the desire for money are causing the chaos and stress in your life. This invocation will help you to refocus your financial perceptions back on spiritual abundance. It will release your thoughts from lack and scarcity. You as a co-creator with God are the source of all abundance. You are freely flowing like the lilies of the fields, and God takes care of your needs. This invocation will remind you of the strong and powerful source of financial blessing that you are. Our worries of lack come from fearful illusions and not from God. With God's love, there is no lack. Financial blessing is an inside job.

Holy Spirit, I ask that you correct my thinking in the areas of money and financial security. Help me to realize that all abundance comes from the divine source within me. Just as I deserve happy and healthy relationships with people, I deserve the same relationship with money. I release all negative programming that blocks me from receiving the bountiful blessings of financial well-being. I know that God provides me with all that I need. Holy Spirit, you know my desires, you know my debts, and you know my fears. I surrender all of these to your creative force. I open my intuitive ear to your direction away from the worry and fear surrounding money. Every step to abundance is guided by your hand. All avenues to financial security are open to me now, and I can feel the stress of lack completely disappear. I switch my thinking from fear to love, and my financial life reflects that miracle. Thank you, Holy Spirit, for I am a lily in the field of life, and all of my needs are met with joy and happiness. Amen.

## INVOCATION OF THE DIVINE ARCHETYPES

In the chapter on spiritual deliverance, I talked about the divine archetypes. Please refer back to that chapter for more information, if desired. This invocation will help you connect to the spiritual resources that vibrate their healing power within you. Divine archetypes may be any spiritual teachers, beings, or masters with whom we find a distinct kinship. Remember that we hold the same vibrational traits of power as the traits that attract us to a divine archetype. Allow this invocation to magnify your connection to specific divine archetypes, and let it help you sustain your daily spiritual practice or balance any life challenges you may be experiencing. Some examples of divine archetypes are Jesus, Buddha, Archangel Michael, Gaia, Krishna, Padre Pio, Joan of Arc, Mother Teresa, and Mother Mary.

Holy Spirit, I ask that you help me open to the divine archetype of (insert name). May I realize that the very power that emanates from this spiritual figure resonates in complete balance with my life. I embody the psychic and spiritual consciousness of (insert name) to help direct my spiritual path. Any challenges I may be experiencing are now enlightened from this sacred union, and I can navigate freely and easily through any situation. I know that I hold the same vibrational power as the divine archetypes you so lovingly place in my life. I am safe—and never alone. May these spiritual resources continuously bless my life. I accept their guidance, realizing that they are a part of my spiritual makeup. Holy Spirit, I thank thee. Amen.

## INVOCATION FOR PSYCHIC INTUITIVE POWER

As you have discovered throughout this book, we are literally be-coming more conscious of our multisensory natures. As we make use of our co-creative natures in the New Golden Age, we must learn that our primary tool while living during this time is our psychic intuitive power. Once we fully engage this essential aspect of our spiritual selves, we will be able to co-create to our highest potential, remaining ever con-scious of those around us who are in need.

> Through the power and grace of the Holy Spirit within me, I open all channels of my psychic intuitive nature. I'm pro-tected and directed by the Christ Consciousness as my mind and heart connect to my higher self, safely engaging the flow of my multisensory self. I listen with clear precision, I see with clear perception, and I act with grace and confidence with the guidance I am given. With the opening of my psy-chic intuitive power, I awaken, transform, and magnify spiri-tual awareness in my life. I make all choices with Divine Love and activate my renewed inner intelligence. Holy Spirit, thank you for this blessing.

## AN EDGAR CAYCE INVOCATION

Following is an invocation given in the Edgar Cayce readings that I have used daily for many years. I believe that this is one of the most powerful invocations that anyone can proclaim for his or her life. If none of the invocations has resonated with you so far, this one is for you. This invocation covers all bases, you might say, and liberates the soul though complete surrender to the Higher Power. I suggest you say this one daily. (As the reading urges: repeat the affirmation, put your trust in Divine Love, and go to work!)

. . . Let my desire and my needs be in Thy hands, Thou
Maker, Creator of the Universe and all the Forces and Powers therein! And may I conform my attitude, my purpose, my
desire, to that Thou hast as an activity for me.

And leave it with Him, and go to work!                462-8

# 10 The Reset Button: The Original Intention of Good

As I bring this work to a close, it is important to understand that your work continues. It is my hope that each chapter and subject has opened a deeper level of awakening within you regarding your destiny. It's imperative that you understand that *you* are the co-creator of your own life. The Divine is with you every day, helping you to realize your limitless potential of creation.

Each chapter and lesson offered in this book is a catalyst for you to allow and receive Divine Love. You have learned to use love's power not only to heal your life but also to help others heal their lives. Each of us was born from light. That light is still as pure and as strong as it was the moment God "thought" us into creation. Creation is all around us; it's what we are made of. How could we possibly be lost in the world when we are literally attached to the most incredible mystical reality of Divine Love? Only our thoughts of separation prevent us from knowing and experiencing our light. Peace, safety, and abundant living are but a thought away. One positive thought can unlock the door to your potential for a better life—the life you were born to live.

As we were expanded from its being, the Creator set the ultimate intention of good for all of us. We have chosen to find other means of union over the ages, and now we are realizing that it is only the Creator's good that offers true and authentic living. We must retune our own personal intentions to the ultimate intention of the Creator's highest good for us. When we "reset" our lives back to the light within–the light as the ultimate good–we are plugging back into the sustained energy that will allow us to co-create for the rest of our physical existence and beyond.

There are times in our life in which we become overwhelmed and bombarded by too much information. Life is sometimes saturated by our own issues, often along with the issues of others, also. During those times, we need to push our reset button. As with any technological device, there are reset buttons to employ when the system becomes stuck. To a degree, we have a similar system. We can energetically reset ourselves back to our original ideal. Our "default factory program" is that of the Creator's original intention of good for us. When we reset our life, we wipe the slate clean and begin again, refreshed and ready to move forward. Resetting does not take away your life lessons. It simply resets your perception by reinforcing your true nature, right mind, and right action in line with the ultimate good. This resetting idea can help you to get back on the horse and ride again. With all of the exercises, prayers, and resources in this book, you may find that you are unable to sense which one you need at a particular time in your life. That is the time to reset. Start again, and refresh your mind.

## PRAYER TO RESET OURSELVES TO THE CREATOR'S ORIGINAL INTENTION OF GOOD

Holy Spirit, I know that my ultimate reality is that of the Creator's good. I ask that you please reset all of my intentions to this good. I now allow the Creator's good intentions for my life to be activated.
I reset my mind to the Creator's good.
I reset my heart to the Creator's good.
I reset my body to the Creator's good
I reset my emotions to the Creator's good.
I reset my life and my destiny to the Creator's good.
Divine Holy Spirit, I thank you for this good. Amen.

# Afterword

**D**ear reader, I want to personally thank you for delving into this subject matter with me. Some of it may have hit home, and some of it may have been hard to digest. Your Higher Self simply needs to take the information that is just right for you at this time. I don't want you to feel like you have to be doing everything *right* in your life. By whose standards is it right, anyway? Do everything in your life as a mindful, conscious being. Just *flow* with the creative force that has been activated in you while reading these pages. You have been given a refresher course, intense as it is. You are ready to embody your true nature as a *Master of Light*. Use this book frequently as a reference or for inspiration. Our earth's energy is shifting for us, so if we keep rising higher and higher in our own spiritual evolution, the earth's energy will vibrate right along with us. Someday, we will see the full reality of the New Golden Age existing all around us. We will have helped to make that happen. What a beautiful thought!

Until that time, know that your own reality—your own world that you are co-creating on a daily basis—is very important to the direction of our united destiny. Stay in the light, make it your own, and always remember to co-create with the hand of God guiding you. Listen to your intuition, let your heart be your sail, and let the Holy Spirit's breath of life take you home to yourself. It is you, and only you, who can co-create your life. You are a Master of Light.

# Resources

## Recommended Web sites

*A Course in Miracles:* www.ACIM.org

Edgar Cayce's A.R.E.: www.EdgarCayce.org

Helen Reddy: www.HelenReddy.com

Ron Roth and Celebrating Life Ministries: www.RonRoth.com

Lindsay Wagner: www.LindsayWagnerInternational.com

Dee Wallace: www.IamDeeWallace.com

## Recommended Books
### *(See also: Bibliography)*

Grant, Robert J. *Edgar Cayce on Angels, Archangels, and the Unseen Forces.* Virginia Beach, VA: A.R.E. Press, 2005.

Reddy, Helen. *The Woman I Am.* Los Angeles: Tarcher Books, 2006.

Roth, Ron, PhD. *Holy Spirit: The Boundless Energy of God.* Carlsbad, CA: Hay House Inc., 2000.

Wagner, Lindsay. "Open to Oneness." Santa Cruz, CA: All Planet Studios, 2009, Audio CD.

Wallace, Dee. *Bright Light: Spiritual Lessons from a Life in Acting.* New Alresford, UK: John Hunt Publishing, 2011.

# Bibliography

*A Course in Miracles*, Combined Volume, Third Edition. Mill Valley, CA: Foundation for Inner Peace, 1976.

Campbell, Joseph, ed. *The Portable Jung.* New York: Penguin Books, 1971.

Cayce, Hugh Lynn. *Venture Inward: Edgar Cayce's Story and the Mysteries of the Unconscious Mind.* Virginia Beach, VA: A.R.E. Press, 1996, (reprinted from New York: Harper & Row, 1964).

Owens, Darrin William. *Reader of Hearts: The Life and Teachings of a Reluctant Psychic.* Novato, CA: New World Library, 2006.

Puryear, Herbert B., PhD. *The Edgar Cayce Primer: Discovering the Path to Self Transformation.* New York: Bantam Books, 1985.

———. *Edgar Cayce: Reflections on the Path.* New York: Bantam Books, 1986.

Roth, Ron, PhD. *Prayer and the Five Stages of Healing.* Carlsbad, CA: Hay House, 1999.

# 4TH DIMENSION PRESS

## An Imprint of A.R.E. Press

4th Dimension Press is an imprint of A.R.E. Press, the publishing division of Edgar Cayce's Association for Research and Enlightenment (A.R.E.).

We publish books, DVDs, and CDs in the fields of intuition, psychic abilities, ancient mysteries, philosophy, comparative religious studies, personal and spiritual development, and holistic health.

For more information, or to receive a catalog, contact us by mail, phone, or online at:

**4th Dimension Press**
215 67th Street
Virginia Beach, VA 23451-2061
800-333-4499

**4THDIMENSIONPRESS.COM**

## Who Was Edgar Cayce?
### Twentieth Century Psychic and Medical Clairvoyant

Edgar Cayce (pronounced Kay-Cee, 1877-1945) has been called the "sleeping prophet," the "father of holistic medicine," and the most-documented psychic of the 20th century. For more than 40 years of his adult life, Cayce gave psychic "readings" to thousands of seekers while in an unconscious state, diagnosing illnesses and revealing lives lived in the past and prophecies yet to come. But who, exactly, was Edgar Cayce?

Cayce was born on a farm in Hopkinsville, Kentucky, in 1877, and his psychic abilities began to appear as early as his childhood. He was able to see and talk to his late grandfather's spirit, and often played with "imaginary friends" whom he said were spirits on the other side. He also displayed an uncanny ability to memorize the pages of a book simply by sleeping on it. These gifts labeled the young Cayce as strange, but all Cayce really wanted was to help others, especially children.

Later in life, Cayce would find that he had the ability to put himself into a sleep-like state by lying down on a couch, closing his eyes, and folding his hands over his stomach. In this state of relaxation and meditation, he was able to place his mind in contact with all time and space—the universal consciousness, also known as the super-conscious mind. From there, he could respond to questions as broad as, "What are the secrets of the universe?" and "What is my purpose in life?" to as specific as, "What can I do to help my arthritis?" and "How were the pyramids of Egypt built?" His responses to these questions came to be called "readings," and their insights offer practical help and advice to individuals even today.

The majority of Edgar Cayce's readings deal with holistic health and the treatment of illness. Yet, although best known for this material, the sleeping Cayce did not seem to be limited to concerns about the physical body. In fact, in their entirety, the readings discuss an astonishing 10,000 different topics. This vast array of subject matter can be narrowed down into a smaller group of topics that, when compiled together, deal with the following five categories: (1) Health-Related Information; (2) Philosophy and Reincarnation; (3) Dreams and Dream Interpretation; (4) ESP and Psychic Phenomena; and (5) Spiritual Growth, Meditation, and Prayer.

Learn more at EdgarCayce.org.

## What Is A.R.E.?

**Edgar Cayce** founded the non-profit Association for Research and Enlightenment (A.R.E.) in 1931, to explore spirituality, holistic health, intuition, dream interpretation, psychic development, reincarnation, and ancient mysteries—all subjects that frequently came up in the more than 14,000 documented psychic readings given by Cayce.

The Mission of the A.R.E. is to help people transform their lives for the better, through research, education, and application of core concepts found in the Edgar Cayce readings and kindred materials that seek to manifest the love of God and all people and promote the purposefulness of life, the oneness of God, the spiritual nature of humankind, and the connection of body, mind, and spirit.

With an international headquarters in Virginia Beach, Va., a regional headquarters in Houston, regional representatives throughout the U.S., Edgar Cayce Centers in more than thirty countries, and individual members in more than seventy countries, the A.R.E. community is a global network of individuals.

A.R.E. conferences, international tours, camps for children and adults, regional activities, and study groups allow like-minded people to gather for educational and fellowship opportunities worldwide.

A.R.E. offers membership benefits and services that include a quarterly body-mind-spirit member magazine, *Venture Inward*, a member newsletter covering the major topics of the readings, and access to the entire set of readings in an exclusive online database.

Learn more at EdgarCayce.org.

# EDGARCAYCE.ORG